Jesus Our Future

Jesus Our Future
Prayers for the Twenty-first Century

Bruce D. Prewer

Ideas into Books®
WESTVIEW
Kingston Springs, Tennessee USA

First edition published 1998 Openbook Publishers

Second edition published May 2014
Ideas into Books®
W E S T V I E W
P.O. Box 605
Kingston Springs, TN 37082
www.publishedbywestview.com

ISBN 978-1-62880-032-6

Printed in the United States of America on acid free paper.

To the ordinary people
of many congregations
who stake their life on Christ

INTRODUCTION

What will the twenty-first century be like? None of us can accurately predict the future. We may project from the present, make educated guesses or build computer models. But we do not know with any certainty.

There will always be many hidden factors at work. Some of them will be benevolent, small flutterings of hope and courage and love, which, like butterfly wings, may produce unexpected achievement and joy. Also there will be hidden viruses of evil, which further down the track may explode with chaos, corruption and suffering.

Given such unpredictability, for a person to write prayers for the third millennium (while one is still living out the last of the second millennium) may seem foolish or pretentious, or maybe (please God) an act of faith.

No matter what else happens, there is and will be a constant, reliable dynamic: the grace of our Lord Jesus Christ, the love of God, and the fellowship of the Holy Spirit. Nothing can take place which can alter this sure thing. No new knowledge can make it obsolete. No foul evil can eliminate it.

Within this holy dynamic, the third millennium will see prayer and praise, sin and forgiveness. There will be worship and witness, fellowship, service and maybe persecutions. There will be surprise and fresh joys, big leaps forward, yet also much stumbling and some sorrows. And, best of all, there will be grace upon grace.

I pray, by that Generosity which works all things together for good for those who love God, that this volume of prayers may assist some pilgrims of the twenty-first century to travel well, to the glory of God.

Bruce D Prewer
5 Laureate Close
Sunbury, Victoria

CONTENTS

ENDING AND BEGINNING

ENDING AND BEGINNING

ᔕᔕᔕ

Saying Goodbye

Leader: Most loving God, we gather to say farewell to a busy century in which we have known much goodness and joy but also much evil and misery.

People: *Help us today to let go of the twentieth century without either glamorising or deriding it, trusting the inexhaustible grace of Christ Jesus to enable us to use the best and discard the worst.*

Leader: We join our prayers, gracious God, with the church that has served before us and the church that will come after us.

People: *O Lord, direct and guide your church with your unfailing care, that it may be diligent in times of quiet and daring in times of trouble. Through Jesus Christ our Lord. Amen.*

Franciscan Breviary (c AD 1226)

Millennium Bug

Lord of history, you will come to judge the living and the dead. Keep us by your grace. In spite of false prophets, bitten by some religious millennium bug, let us be good stewards of the gospel of peace and lively shareholders in the Spirit. Do not allow newly awakened fears and anxieties to cast out love and trust, nor shrill voices predicting an imminent Second Coming to distract us from loving our neighbour today. Encourage us to live each day calmly, hopefully, courageously and creatively, knowing that all things are in your sure hands. Constantly give us the unflustered sanity of those who know that they are saved by grace. Then, at your coming, whenever it may be, we will be ready. Through Jesus Christ our Saviour. Amen.

Thanks for the Memories

God our help in ages past, we leave behind the old century with gratitude and thanksgiving for all achievements and remarkable individuals:

We praise and thank you, source of all joy.

For the increased possibilities for good health: antibiotics and vaccinations, hearing aids and pacemakers, gentle anaesthetics and open-heart surgery, dietary knowledge and radiology:

We praise and thank you, source of good health.

For advances in technology: telephone and motor cars, transistor radios and television, automatic teller machines and aeroplanes, CAT scans and radio telescopes, computers and washing machines:

We praise and thank you, source of innovation.

For agencies that reach out in love to the needy: Red Cross and Amnesty International, Community Aid Abroad and World Vision, Australian Volunteers Abroad and our Flying Doctor Service:

We praise and thank you, source of compassion.

For the renewal of your church: the ecumenical healing of divisions and the struggles for social justice, fresh liturgies and the outpouring of new hymns, charismatic movements and house churches:

We praise and thank you, source of rebirth.

For your special people who have inspired us: John Flynn and Helen Keller, Pope John XXIII and Martin Luther King, Karl Barth and Mother Teresa, Billy Graham and Desmond Tutu:

We praise and thank you, source of the saints.

For all who adored the God of steadfast love,

for all who trusted the grace of Christ Jesus,

for all who delighted in the fellowship of the Holy Spirit,

we praise and thank you, God of the twentieth century!

Amen!

Amen!

Litany of Repentance

Leader: As typical citizens of the Australian nation, let us repent of both the individual and corporate evil that has afflicted us during this century.

People: *Loving God, friend and saviour, we confess the sins which have infected and blighted our lifestyle and alienated us from each other and from you.*

Leader: We repent of the racism, sometimes open, sometimes furtive, which has increased the loneliness and misery of minority groups.

People: *We confess our reluctance to understand or alleviate the pain of Indigenous people. We repent of the massacres which took place early this century and the present-day evasions and injustices.*

Leader: We repent of our ignorant and at times wilful abuse of the land and its creatures and our despoiling of the soil, air and water.

People: *We confess the destruction of forests, the depletion of the ozone layer, the extinction of unique animals, the salination of large tracts of land, and the pollution of river systems.*

Leader: We repent of our past arrogance towards the races of the Pacific Islands and South East Asia.

People: *We confess to hiding behind the infamous White Australia Policy, exploiting Papua New Guinea, resenting Asian refugees, and using aid for political purposes.*

Leader: We repent of our apathy and sometimes scorn towards the unemployed and the unemployable.

People: *We confess the sin of condemning youth to frustration and futility and discarding loyal employees in their fifties.*

Leader: We repent of our slide into opinion-poll morality, the cult of self-indulgence, and taxation by casino and poker machine.

People: *We confess the politics of expediency, the lack of prophetic courage, the use of the media for mass lying.*

Leader: We confess a legal system that favours the rich and a church culture that favours the respectable.

People: *We repent of our neglect of prayer, Scripture, social justice issues and evangelism and our reluctance to make friends among the disreputable for Christ's sake.*

Leader: Lord have mercy.   **People:** *Lord have mercy.*

Leader: Christ have mercy.   **People:** *Christ have mercy.*

Leader: Lord have mercy.   **People:** *Lord have mercy.*

Announcement of Forgiveness

Leader: My friends, step free from the dark face of the past and turn to the light and hope of tomorrow. Listen to the gospel: God did not send his Son into the world to condemn this century but in order that through Christ this world might be saved. You are a much loved and forgiven people!

People: *Thanks be to God!*

For Better, for Worse

I bless you, my Friend, for all that you have given me and all that you have taken from me. You are indeed a God of love. Be with me, Lord, for the time to come. Keep me close to you, day by day, night by night, and take away everything that hinders me from being altogether yours. Amen.

Ashton Oxenden (19th century, Canada)

In Changing Times

When world events seem to spin so fast
that I am afraid of losing my foothold,
when the rate of change tosses me about
like bulldust in a willy-willy,
 come to me, O Spirit of quietness,
 and gather me up into the great stillness
 of your unflappable love, joy and peace.
 Through Jesus Christ our Lord.
Amen.

Drastic Faithfulness

God of faithfulness, by your tireless Spirit infiltrate the days
and years of this young millennium with the vibrant leaven of
Christ Jesus. Fulfil in and through us your promises, that we
may draw nearer to that time when the earth shall be filled
with the glory of the Lord as the waters cover the sea.

Inspire in us a faith which takes bolder steps than the petty
shuffling of mere credulity. Instil in us the grace to stop short
and turn back, when that is the only way by which we may go
forward in the Spirit of Christ.

In your name and for your glory. Amen.

Jesus Our Future

Lord Jesus, you come like a genius,
like someone far ahead of their time.
You come as a miracle,
not breaking the laws of nature but fulfilling them.

You are the future towards which the Spirit draws us,
the salvation offered to all humanity,
the joy exceeding all exciting pleasures,
the destiny that was prepared for us
before the foundation of the world.

You come as the humble Perfection outside our grasp
yet graciously within our reach.
You are the Beauty that is to come,
the Beauty that calls us into that most natural
of all miracles: the ministry of love.

O God's unique genius, we welcome you
as Saviour, Friend and Lord. Amen.

A Creed for Now

We believe in the loving Creator,

whose generous providence has been above all, beneath all and in all the moments and days of this twentieth century, and will be at work in ages to come.

We believe in Jesus Christ,

whose saving grace finds, heals and reconciles millions of lost sinners, including even us, and who calls us to the ministry of reconciliation.

We believe in the Spirit of truth,

whose tireless energy is at work through all the upheavals, achievements, disappointments, joys and discoveries of this era.

We believe in this wonderful God,

who loves our land and its people and is weaving through the tangled affairs of our nation a purpose outreaching anything we could imagine.

We believe that our belief is a precious gift,

to be treasured, nurtured, shared and dared to the praise and glory of God forever.

Amen and Amen!

Approaching 2000

Wonderful God, while we wait for the third millennium, some of us expect too much while others expect too little. Saviour-friend, drive from us the childishness that frets for signs and wonders; tear from us the cynicism which barricades the soul against renewal.

Muscle in with your healthy Spirit, that we may willingly attempt new patterns of thinking, serving and worshipping. Toughen our faith to take risks for you, and grant us the grace to make mistakes to your glory! Give us the resilience to rise up from setbacks with an Easter eagerness and a Pentecost impertinence!

From the rising of the sun to its going down may your name be great among the nations! Amen!

Creatures of Time

O Lord of time and eternity, you make us creatures of time that, when time is over, we may attain your blessed eternity. With time as your gift, give us also wisdom to redeem the time, lest our day of grace be lost. For our Lord Jesus Christ's sake. Amen.

Christina Rossetti (1830–94)

Young Again

Loving God, make your world-wide church young again. Let us, with adolescent vigour, expect plenty from Christ and expend plenty for Christ.

Do not permit the memory of the follies of the last century to stifle or distort our hope for these new times.

Put paid to our fears and give us far more than we bargained for, so that something of your kingdom, power and glory may be displayed in us.

Through Jesus Christ our Lord. Amen.

Our Times

Lord of flowing times and seasons,
of minutes, centuries and millennia,
a hundred years in your sight are less
than the blinking of an eye.

We realise that our fascination
with calendars and centuries
displays our human insecurity
and brief tenure in this world.

Have pity on our vulnerability.
Humour and guide us as we begin
to explore this brand new century,
which to us seems momentous.

Let it not be a pathetic regurgitation
of our past follies and failures.
Reinvigorate the quality of our loving
and help us keep faith with your kingdom.

Heroic Love

O you who are heroic love, keep alive in our hearts that adventurous spirit which makes your people scorn the way of safety, so that your will be done. For so only, O Lord, shall we be worthy of those courageous souls who in every age have ventured all in obedience to your call, and for whom the trumpets have sounded on the other side; through Jesus Christ our Lord. Amen.

John Oldham

Past and Future

Divine Friend, you never vary in your loving faithfulness and you never weary of making all things new.
Guide us through these changing times.

Do not permit our outlook to be ruled by anxiety
or subverted by sentimental nostalgia.
Do not allow us to live in the museum of the past
or to neglect its hard but enlightening lessons.
Do not let us live in daydreams about the future
or neglect its exciting opportunities.
For your love's sake. Amen.

The Next Step

As we step over the ridge of the twentieth century and confront virgin territory, save us from both the clutch of anxiety and the itch for novelty.

Give us the faith to explore new possibilities with willing feet and open eyes. Show us also that your word has not grown old and your grace has not become exhausted. With the wise who have lived before us and with those who will come after us we pray the pilgrim's prayer: 'Lead us in the paths of righteousness for your name's sake'.

By your unbound Spirit of truth,
liberate us to seize fresh opportunities,
following the lead of our Saviour, Christ,
the same yesterday, today and forever.
For your love's sake. Amen.

Followers

Holy Spirit, Soul of Love,
unleash your abundance within me
until every faculty is transfused
with your healing immensity,
    that I may have the vision
    to discern the footprints of Christ
    in this twenty-first century
    and possess the love and courage
    to follow wherever he leads me.
To the praise
    of the Name that is timeless
and to the glory
    of the Love that is boundless.
Amen.

Divine Gamble

God, make each moment of our lives a miracle. God, make us laugh at the impossible. God, give us hope when all seems hopeless, peace where no peace could be, love for the unlovable. Make us gamble on all your almightiness and dare everything in your great service. Amen.

M E Procter (20th century)

Where Are We Heading?

Lord of history, Lord of our days, discourage us from buying the fashionable myth that things are getting better and better.

Give us a view of the future which has nothing to do with the puerile propaganda of progress. Give us persistent faith in the ongoing redeeming work of Christ Jesus. Remind us each morning of your ability to bring good out of evil and rebirth out of death. Let us know and trust the Spirit, who neither faints nor grows weary.

Show us the next steps we can take. When we stumble, let us not be discouraged, as long as we have stumbled while walking your paths. Through Jesus Christ our Lord. Amen.

God of Space Shuttles

God of office towers and space shuttles,
of peak-hour traffic and the Milky Way,
   help us to seek you.

God of city hospitals and flying doctors,
of intensive care and desert sunsets,
   help us to find you.

God of noisy airports and outback tracks,
of control towers and red kangaroos,
   help us to know you.

God of pop concerts and country shows,
of violin concertos and cooing doves,
   help us to trust you.

God of football crowds and lone yachts,
of protest marches and moonlit waves,
   help us to love you.

God of cathedral choirs and corroborees,
of Lifeline counsellors and birdsong at dawn,
   help us to serve you.

God of Mary's son and Peter's Lord,
of a bloody cross and an empty tomb,
   help us to adore you.

New Things

Spirit of truth, do not let us hide behind locked doors, afraid
of every new idea and prejudiced against all new theories.

Rather, let our minds be constantly tuned with the gospel of
Christ Jesus and then be open to explore fresh ideas with
sanctified curiosity.

Count us among those wise and adventurous souls who 'bring
from their storeroom things old and things new'. To your
endless wonder and worship. Amen.

Blind Faith

Spirit of Christ,

we, who like to think
we are reasonable people
of scientific bent,
thank you for the gift

of blind faith.

Where we can no longer see
but stand bemused and hope-less,
you come to our side
and give us the courage

to leap

across a love-gulf so deep
that it separates
Dives from Lazarus
and despair from joy.

Spirit of Christ,

stand by us today,
that we may again leap
where reason fears to tread
and love where ego stalls.

A New Vision for a New Age

*O God, our Shepherd, give to the church a new vision and a
new charity, new wisdom and fresh understanding, the revival of
her brightness and the renewal of her unity, that the eternal
message of your Son, undefiled by human traditions, may be
hailed as the good news of the new age; through him who
makes all things new, Jesus Christ our Lord. Amen.*

Percy Dearmer (1867–1936)

Live for the Moment?

Maker of time, God of eternity, we cannot take the advice of those twenty-first century gurus who tell us to live only for the moment. Because you have taught us to look back to a cross and the Person of remarkable grace, the past is not a dead hand inhibiting us but a source of freedom and joy. Because you enable us to look forward to the coming again of the Person of remarkable grace, the future is neither threat nor chance but promise and opportunity.

Between the glory that was and the glory that is to come assist each of us, God of eternity, to live each day with a free and disciplined love, trusting that remarkable grace which overflows each moment with a joy far superior to any treasure we could plan or bargain for.

In the name of the Father, Son, and Holy Spirit. Amen.

Rafting

Take us, adventurous Saviour,
from the polluted backwaters
of common indifference
to the fierce, white waters of your love.

Let us ride the raft of faith
joyfully, without looking back,
willing to work as a team
with those who adventure with us.

Use what strengths we have
for the good of all.
Give us the humility to allow others
to cover for our weaknesses.

On currents of turbulent providence
bring us to the camping place
which you have in store for us,
and there let us rest in your peace.

For your love's sake. Amen.

For Our Nation

Lord of all races and nations, we thank you for our country and its people, our blessings and our privileges. By your Holy Spirit lead us through the new millennium with both humility and confidence.

Though we are small among the nations, teach us to do justly, love mercy and walk humbly with our God.

Move with your renewing Spirit of wisdom in the hearts and minds of our prime minister and our state premiers. May they not only have the will to seek the common good but also the wisdom to recognise what truly is the common good.

Though we are small among the nations, teach us to do justly, love mercy, and walk humbly with our God.

By your Spirit of truth, discipline the minds of those who edit and control our mass media. Give them the courage to spurn the sensational gossip and the violence which tears the fabric of our society yet publish the truth that cleanses and builds up.

Though we are small among the nations, teach us to do justly, love mercy, and walk humbly with our God.

Come with your compassionate Spirit on all those who help mend the wounds and ills of our society: those who reach out to street kids and drug addicts, all who care for misfits and outcasts, those who tend the diseased and injured, and all brave souls who try to right wrongs by changing unjust attitudes and laws.

Though we are small among the nations, teach us to do justly, love mercy and walk humbly with our God.

By your reconciling Spirit, bridge the gap between city and country, the employed and the unemployed, the wealthy and the battlers, Indigenous Australians and more recent generations of immigrants, the political right and political left, the powerful and the weak.

Though we are small among the nations, teach us to do justly, love mercy and walk humbly with our God.

Pour out the Spirit of Christ Jesus upon the congregations of your church in this land. Encourage and renew your ministers, pastors and priests. Raise up prophets and evangelists of small ego and mighty faith. Let this new era be a time of opportunity that is faithfully seized in the name of your true Son.

Though we are small among the nations, teach us to do justly, love mercy and walk humbly with our God.

Loving God, through Christ Jesus who strengthens us, we commit ourselves to making this new century a place where grace, mercy and peace are not in short supply.

In the all-providing, liberating and revitalising name of the Father, Son and Holy Spirit. Amen.

Commanded to Hope

In a world that selfishly lives for the moment, without thought for whatever evil we may be causing the future, we thank you, God, for commanding us to be people of hope.

Do not allow us to be conformed to the present short-sighted, self-serving attitudes but open our eyes to see all those things that are possible through Christ Jesus our Saviour.

Give us a sure commitment to your new heaven and new earth by living some of the promised future in the here and now:
giving with no thought of reward
reaching out to the forsaken
bandaging the wounded
challenging injustices
fostering seeds of faith
caring for mother earth
exposing pride and greed
building bridges of understanding
and loving our neighbours of the future.
Stretch our vision to include the improbable and strengthen our wills to take the next step on your road. Assure us again that you can do exceedingly more than we can ever ask or imagine.

Glory be to your loving purposes, now and forever! Amen.

New Discoveries

We become caught up, Lord of life, in the media hype
which follows each discovery or breakthrough
of this glittering era.

We get excited about
    the new cures for diseases that have long afflicted us
    the fresh theories about the origins of humanity
    the latest surprise from space probes
    the most recent high-tech surgery
    new insights into how our brain works
    the latest generation of fruits and flowers
    the state-of-the-art wizardry from 'silicon valley'.

Yet, a few months further on, we try to remember
what all the hype was about.

God of majestic, awesome, inexpressible glory,
do not allow us to become so jaded by innovation
that we forget the ever-present miracle of your incarnate,
redeeming love in Christ Jesus, who is making all things new.
Amen.

FACING UP
TO OURSELVES

FACING UP
TO OURSELVES

Unreal, Man, Unreal!

Plain-speaking Christ, teller of truth, friend of the pure in heart, we confess that we exchange reality for the glossy unreal!

Through the tricks of the film maker, the intermingling of fact and fantasy, the juxtaposition of cartoon and living actor, we lose ourselves in illusions.

> Lord have mercy. *Christ have mercy.*

Through the pernicious deceits of the advertising industry, making us puppets of fashion in food, clothing, motor cars and entertainment.

> Lord have mercy. *Christ have mercy.*

Through the subverting of human dignity by which children become 'the market', voters are numbers, and sexual promiscuity is called 'making love'.

> Lord have mercy. *Christ have mercy.*

Through the technology of modern warfare, where fellow human beings become mere target positions on video screens.

> Lord have mercy. *Christ have mercy.*

Through the marketing of religion as consumer goods, where the clients become the centre and worship is tailored to fit our current wants, where wonder, awe, honest doubt, cost and discipline are sacrificed to accessible triviality.

> Lord have mercy. *Christ have mercy.*

The Laser of God

Christ Jesus,
laser of the living God,
light of this spinning planet,
 pierce the clouds of our ignorance,
 correct the distortion in our vision,
 lance the abscess of our self-interest,
 cut away the scar tissue of old hurts,
 cauterise the weeping sores of our discontents,
 and give us a much-needed faith-lift.
We place ourselves in your unshakeable hands
for whatever radical surgery you choose.

Lord have mercy.   *Lord have mercy.*

Christ have mercy.   *Christ have mercy.*

Lord have mercy.   *Lord have mercy.*

You, God, are the light of the minds that know you, the joy of the hearts that love you, and the strength of the wills that serve you. Grant us so to know you that we may truly love you, and so to love you that we may fully serve you, whom to serve is perfect freedom, in Jesus Christ our Lord. Amen.

St Augustine of Hippo (AD 354–430)

What We Really Need

God of Christ Jesus and our God, how profoundly we need you! We need you in our weaknesses, we need you when we think we are strong.

We need
 to return from our wanderings to your eternal at-home-ness
 to relax our tense self-importance in your huge humility
 to review our cleverness in the light of your wisdom
 to repair our brokenness in your perfect wholeness
 to rest our pettiness in the wonder of your immensity
 to restore our tired love in your inexhaustible grace.

God of Christ Jesus, we need you far more than we can ever estimate. Gather us up in your warmth and answer the prayers of our recognised and unrecognised needs.

For your love's sake. Amen.

Too Much and Too Little

Divine Friend, have mercy on your children who suffer both from too much and too little.

Lord, have mercy. Christ, have mercy. Lord, have mercy.

We are the unbalanced people, the creatures whose riches are their pathetic poverty:

we crowd our homes with possessions, but we are tragically short on love;

we gaze transfixed at electronic images yet rarely look into human eyes;

we spawn regulations and laws, yet we discount individual integrity;

we stagger under a load of information but lack common sense;

we have plenty of preachers but not enough humble practitioners;

we organise armies of advisers, yet there is a drastic shortage of wisdom;

we rush around like tourists but neglect to take time to become pilgrims;

we have swapped the peace of one God for a legion of bedevilled voices.

Lord, have mercy. Christ, have mercy. Lord, have mercy.

O son of Mary, you practised what you preached, you loved far past the limits of your understanding, you embodied the God in whom you trusted. Christ Jesus, please dare to be embodied in us. Take charge of our cluttered yet empty lives and bring us back to the divine simplicities of faith, hope and love. Amen.

Make Me

Lord, make me like a crystal, that your light may shine through me. Amen.

Katherine Mansfield (1888–1923)

The Virus in Our Systems

Our God, you who wear our bruises and carry our sins, we find it difficult not to be discouraged by the virus of evil which seems to be out of control, affecting all our systems. Each exciting advance which humanity makes soon becomes corrupted. Our best technology, our new political parties, our bold surges in spirituality are infected by ancient strains of evil in modern forms.

To struggle against it, dear God, and to maintain our integrity and enthusiasm, seems a tall order. Sometimes we feel close to the ancient cry of frustration: 'Futility of futilities! All is futility!'*

Come to our aid, Saviour of old! Come and help us, Saviour of the future! Bring us again to the mighty, inverse power of your cross. Show us once more the tomb which cannot keep you in, and the locked room which cannot keep out your risen presence. Impel us with the love which comes like a rushing wind and tongues of fire.

O source and goal of a new age yet to be fulfilled, teach us to trust you far more than we fear evil. Inspire us to live faithfully, freely and joyfully, believing that nothing done in your name can ever be futile.

We ask this in the name which is far above all other names. Amen.

* Ecclesiastes 1:2

Hard-headed Mercy

O Saviour Christ, come among us with your hard-headed mercy and startling paradoxes. Shatter our illusions before they become our damnation. Call us back to the worship of one God. Energise us and align us with the Spirit of truth. Fill us with that costly grace which shows its true colours on your awful yet wonderful cross.

Astronauts

Watch over us, eternal God, as we hurtle through space on the way to things the mind has not yet dreamed of.

Help us to deal kindly with one another in this confined space, to be patient with each other's frailties, to forgive those who sin against us, to treasure our neighbour's abilities, and to rejoice in each other's achievements.

Teach us to share the provisions fairly, to bear the workload evenly, and to deal as justly with the most lowly ranked among us as we would with the captain. Let us encourage each other to take time to watch the stars, to marvel at the work of your fingers, and to worship without pretence.

Then, Lord, as this spaceship Earth continues on its long voyage, may we be ready to inherit the world that is to come. Through Jesus Christ our Lord. Amen.

Minor Miracle Workers?

Have pity, loving God, on a race which achieves minor miracles yet progresses very little.

We can restore sight, move mountains, fly through space, yet we have not learnt how to share our daily bread.

We make deserts blossom as the rose and implant new valves in hearts, yet we cannot live together in peace.

We can speak to each other across vast distances and sometimes even wake the dead, but we do not love one another.

Lord, have mercy.   *Lord, have mercy.*

Christ, have mercy.   *Christ, have mercy.*

Lord, have mercy.   *Lord, have mercy.*

Rescue us from the enigma of our own being. Heal our divided nature. Give us the desire and the will to be saved. Help us to reach towards that wholeness and joy which you have prepared for those who love you. For your love's sake. Amen.

Searcher of Hearts

O Searcher of hearts, you know us better than we know
ourselves. You see the sins which our very sinfulness hides from
our eyes. Lift us up from where we have fallen. Keep us from sin
in all we do today. Fill us with a holy simplicity, content to seek
and do your will. Through Jesus Christ our Lord. Amen.

J Martineau (1805–1900)

Cockroaches

God of Jesus Christ, we dare to be honest with you as we dare
not be with anyone else, not even our dearest friends. It is a
relief to confess the ugly side of our nature. Beneath the veneer
of our modern sophistication, under the thin veil of our
tenuous faith and goodness, there lurk repulsive thoughts,
feelings and motives, the cockroaches of the soul, which hide
in the murky crevices of our minds.

We do not want them, but they are in us, Lord. Occasionally
we come face to face with brazen ones, like racism or greed,
and we are appalled by the perverse allure of evil. More often
we see them only in our peripheral vision as they scuttle for
their hiding places, not wanting to be identified.

Merciful God, we fear this subterranean part of our nature, the
realm where the prince of darkness has access. We recognise
that there is only a thin line between our sophistication and all
the cruel and disgusting evils in the world.

O Saviour God, we beg you to save us from both the evil
without and the potential evil within us. Keep us honest with
ourselves. Keep us alert to what is happening within us, that
we may not blind ourselves with pious pretensions and fall
victim to the evils of which we are all capable.

May the grace of our Lord Jesus Christ make us more than
conquerors, through him who loves us. Amen.

For Deliverance

O God, source of rescue and healing, deliver us
from the tyrannies of entertainment
    and the glamour of electronic gambling,
from the novelty of internet religions
    and the cosiness of TV Christianity.
God of salvation, deliver us.

From the myopia of the mass media
    and the diet of despair,
from the possessiveness of possessions
    and the lure of the latest sales,
God of salvation, deliver us.

From scientific dogmatism
    and fashionable medicine,
from the creeds of economists
    and the litanies of politicians,
God of salvation, deliver us.

From all that diverts our faith
    and all that dilutes our love,
from a repetition of past sins
    in our new life in Christ Jesus,
God of salvation, deliver us. Amen.

From the Shadowland

On the slagheap
    of accumulated defeats,
plodding days
    of grey despondency,
inhaling the smog
    of stale apathy—

Come, Spirit of the Lord,
    come and rescue us
    from the shadowland.
Come, Spirit of truth,
    with your tough grace,
    your resolute love.
Come, Spirit of Christ,
    and bring us out again
    to the land of laughter.

From Less-than-real

Saviour-Friend, we are weary of virtual reality. Illusions have taken over our leisure, stifled our imagination, blinded us to the needs of others, tutored us to be artificial in intimate relationships, and left us with scant time for wonder and worship.

Come to our aid, Saviour-Friend. Redeem us from bondage to illusions. Save us from everything that is less that real. Deliver us into the naked truth of your Spirit.

Restore in us the aspirations and hungers for which we were created. Let us reclaim the unique reality of our own soul and relate without pretence to the reality of others.

Heal our scarred imagination, so that our young people may see visions of heaven on earth and our old folk dream of a world full-filled with the gospel. To your endless joy and glory. Amen.

A Ransom Note

We plead, loving God, to be ransomed from the counterfeit glory of this self-serving world and placed in the care of your only beloved Son.

From words that babble and confuse, flatter and deceive,
to the Word that is life and health,
ransom us, God of grace and glory.
From lights that strobe and entice, dazzle and blind,
to the Light that searches for the lost,
ransom us, God of grace and glory.
From half-truths that shout and dogmatise, bully and enslave,
to the Truth that is pure liberty,
ransom us, God of grace and glory.
From joys that indulge and tire, distract and cloy,
to the Joy that uplifts and ennobles,
ransom us, God of grace and glory.
From friends that can be won or lost, true or false,
to the Friend of unconditional faithfulness,
ransom us, God of grace and glory.
In the company of our Saviour may we learn that lifestyle which is daily abundant and eternally refulgent with love and praise. Through Jesus Christ our Lord. Amen.

Those Murky Corners

God, penetrate those murky corners where we hide memories, and tendencies on which we do not care to look, but which we will not yield freely to you, that you might purify and transmute them. The persistent buried grudge, the half-acknowledged enmity which is still smouldering, the bitterness of that loss we have not turned into sacrifice, the private comfort we cling to, the secret fear of failure which saps our initiative and is really inverted pride, the pessimism which is an insult to your joy. Lord, we bring all these to you, and we review them with shame and penitence in your steadfast light. Through Jesus Christ our Saviour. Amen.

Evelyn Underhill (1875–1941)

Hallucinations

God of tenacious love, rescue us from the herd mentality of this arrogant century. Save us from all that mesmerises and deludes us.

We confess that we too easily become caught up in the mass hallucinations in which the population lives and moves and has its being:
>   we join in the anxious stampede for money and possessions
>   we enmesh ourselves in the selfishness which exploits the
>   weak
>   we blindly dance to the beat and tune of political parties
>   we pay lip service to the Spirit yet live by the agnosticism of
>   the mob
>   apart from a few religious habits, there is little to mark us
>   out from the scurrying crowd.

God of tenacious love, break through the walls of our false perceptions. Shatter our delusions. Send in your Christ to overthrow the tables, scatter our love of money and drive out the animals from the temple of the human soul. Confront us with the fearful beauty of your pure love. Cleanse us without restraint and open us to the winds of heaven. Being owned by you, may we own ourselves with the joyful liberty of Christ Jesus our Lord. Amen.

When We Are Empty

*Look, Lord, here is an empty mug that needs to be filled. My
Lord, fill it. I am frail in the faith; strengthen me. I am cold in
love; warm me and make me fervent, that my love may reach
out to my neighbour. I do not have a strong and stable faith; at
times I doubt and am unable to trust you completely. O Lord,
help me. Strengthen my faith and trust in you. Amen.*

Martin Luther (1483–1536)

Healthy Desire

Is it you, Lord,
 or the absence of you
    that gnaws at my being
    with unutterable longing?

I know you well,
yet just as surely
    in this dyslectic world
    I know you hardly at all.

You have saved me
from doubt and death,
    but with yearning heart
    I long to be fully saved.

Your peace has knitted
my unravelled soul,
    yet there is holy discontent
    instead of tranquillity.

My restlessness has found
an ultimate rest in you,
    but now no worldly pillow
    gives rest to my head.

Am I to be, Lord God,
a perpetual wanderer,
    like some castaway
    from a distant star?

From Ego-loneliness

We confess, merciful Friend, that many of us have become
lonely islands. Too often we have worshipped at the altar of
individualism and have forfeited the precious gift of
community. We plant our self-interest in friendship and
marriage, religion and politics, employment and leisure and
end up reaping distrust and division.

Saving God, rescue us from our isolation. Awaken in us the
passion for sharing and caring. Inspire us with the love which
breaks out of the narrow lane of individualism into your
thoroughfare, where we can respect, treasure, serve and
enhance other lives.

Return us to that state of grace where we discern the face of
Christ in husband or wife, child or parent, friend or opponent,
employee or employer, neighbour or enemy. Help us to cherish
community and to tap that power and glory which is
wonderfully revealed on a cross.

For your love's sake. Amen.

Astronomical

God of immensities, while astronomers at Parkes or Siding
    Springs
probe more of the mind-blowing majesty of outer space,
save us from writing ourselves off as trivial specks
inhabiting one unimportant little planet.

Remind us that by your grace it is we who are doing the
    probing.
You have chosen us to be creatures of intellect and curiosity.
Through vast stretches of time you have nurtured us
and called us to a special place in this universe,
giving us a spirit which reflects your own.

To complete our high calling and redeem us from outer
    darkness
you have shared our earthy humanity in Jesus the Christ,
taught us that the hairs on our heads are numbered,
and shown us that not even suffering or death
can cut us off from your love.

O God of mighty wonders, intimate details and eternal
    purposes,
encourage us forward into new discoveries and opportunities.
Enable us to humbly wear your gift of high significance,
and to treasure the amazing grace which names us
children of God and joint heirs with Christ.

In his name we pray. Amen.

Virtual Reality

For the gifts of virtual reality
we give you thanks, Lord of all life:
    for the opportunity to hone skills
        and probe new possibilities,
    to discover our own strengths
        and realise our weaknesses;
    when we are wearied by work,
        to be entertained and relaxed;
    when we become judgmental,
        to put ourselves in another's shoes.
Yet we also pray for deliverance
from the snares of virtual reality:
    from the seductions of fiction
        that edge out the disciplines of faith,
    from being immersed in phantasies
        while ignoring our own household,
    from a passion for colourful images
        yet apathy towards our neighbours,
    from living in the fantasy of others
        while denying the visions of the Spirit.
Keep us in touch with your reality, God.
Save us and enhance us by your gospel:
    knit us to your really real Christ,
        that, putting first things first,
    we may seek your unique kingdom
        and its loving righteousness
    and enter into that un-anxious joy
        which has been prepared for us
    by the source of all wonder and light
        since the foundation of the world.
Amen.

When We Serve Idols

God of Mount Sinai and Moses, the fierce enemy of the carved images* which fascinate and corrupt humanity, have mercy on us.

Ours is the golden age of images. We spend our days among an endless electronic supply, which we pretend are there to serve us. But in truth we more often serve them with a devotion far exceeding what we offer you. We have bowed down to our idols, gloried in their artificial worlds, communicated with them far more than we have with our fellows, even neglecting the members of our own households.

We reap the bitter harvest of our idolatry: dysfunctional families, separations, divorce, youth suicides, soulless sex, drugs, and a restless search for some new image that might fill the void at the core of our being.

O God! Before it is too late, put paid to our idols. Shatter our addiction to video screens, keyboards, icons and exotic software. Grind the golden calf of our electronic illusions into an unpalatable dust. Confront us with the glory of your righteous love and awaken in us that first awe and delight which is the indigenous worship of our spirits.

Call us back to the 'true God of true God' and the knowledge that 'you have made us for yourself and our hearts are restless until they find their rest in you'.

For through Christ Jesus, yours is the kingdom of the heart's desire, the power made perfect in human weakness, and the glory which begins now and stretches into the infinitude of forever! Amen!

*See Exodus 32

THANKING
AND
CELEBRATING

THANKING AND CELEBRATING

Cosmic Praise

Lord of all the children of the stars,
in whatever form you have shaped them,
by whatever name they serve you,
help us on this planet Earth, our home,
to keep our minds and hearts attuned
to every pulse of your cosmic Spirit.
Focus our lives on your special visitation
in our Saviour Christ, from whom
nothing in heaven or earth can separate us.
Join our service and our worship
to all the praise that at this moment rises
from loving spirits throughout creation.
For yours is the kingdom,
the power and the glory
forever and everywhere. Amen.

Thanks for Deprivations

Lord, I thank you that in your love you have taken away from me all earthly wealth and that you now clothe and feed me through the kindness of others. Lord, I thank you that since you have taken away the sight of my eyes you serve me now through the eyes of others. Lord, I thank you that since you have taken away the strength of my hands and my heart you minister to me by the hands and hearts of others. Lord, I pray for them. Reward them for it in your heavenly love, that they may faithfully serve and please you till they reach a happy end. Amen.

Mechthild of Magdeburg (1210–c 1280)

New Frontiers

We thank you, God of endless challenges, for those thinkers and explorers who are extending the frontiers of human knowledge:

> biologists, searching genetic codes for ways to eradicate some of our hereditary ills
>
> space scientists and astronauts, taking the first, primitive steps towards finding new worlds
>
> theologians, living on the new borders with the holy Scriptures in their open hands
>
> ecumenical diplomats, willingly spending themselves in the quest for justice and peace
>
> medical researchers, discovering new methods of treatment for human suffering
>
> ethical philosophers, wrestling with moral dilemmas which have never before been faced
>
> computer scientists, striving to harness artificial intelligence for the good of all humanity
>
> preachers, daring to stand on the new territories in the light of the gospel of Christ
>
> agricultural scientists, endeavouring to increase our ability to feed the underfed millions
>
> artists, poets, musicians, exploring the heights and depths of our contemporary experience.

God of truth and grace, for these brave souls we thank you. May they have the wisdom and the humility to 'seek first your kingdom and its right living' and so discover the blessings of the children of God.

Through Jesus Christ, our brother and Lord. Amen.

Cities

Source of life and love, help us to see that cities are as much a part of nature as termite mounds, flocks of corellas and a hives of wild bees.

Free us to exult in the good facets of city life as much as we applaud the virtues of country living. And give us the will and wisdom to improve the quality of both; to fulfil your purposes and glorify your name. Amen.

O Beauty!

O Loveliness! O Beauty excelling beauty!

Because you have touched me,
    freely and unconditionally,
I have sought more of your wonder
    in the colours of this world.

In the melodies and harmonies
    of music I listen for you.
With the poor, the meek and the beggar
    with no name I reach for you.

By outback mountains and rainforest
    streams I wait for you.
Through the world's great galleries
    of art I look for you.

In the latest scientific discovery
    or theory I expect you.
With every new technological
    surprise I search for you.

Among erudite theologies and poetic
    images I hunger for you.
In the disciplines of meditation
    and prayer I wait for you.

But never have I held you,
    except in those awe-moments
when you have found and held me
    with the inexpressible grace of Christ.

O Loveliness! O Beauty excelling beauty!

A Family in One

You, God, are father and mother to me, a brother, a sister, a friend. You manage my house for me. You are all that is, and all that is resides in you. We praise you and thank you, we give you glory, human though we are and weak. You alone are God for all eternity! Amen.

Acts of Peter (AD 180–190)

God of Merriment

God of merriment, for whom the morning stars sing together and all the children of God shout for joy, help us keep our sense of humour.

When those around us get hyped-up about the latest scientific discovery or technological wizardry, help us to see the comical side of human self-importance.

When we take ourselves too seriously, as if the church were built on our devout efforts, enable us to chuckle at our folly.

When evil parades itself in finery and thinks it owns the world, or when untimely death appears to cut off saints in their prime, fill us with the robust joy of Easter.

God of 'solid joys and lasting pleasures', because of all your victories in Christ Jesus, liberate us to share in the song of the morning stars and the joyful shouts of the children of God, today and forevermore. Amen.

Holiday

Instead of the roar of motor cars,
    the rhythmic pulse of the sea.
Instead of the radio's traffic report,
    the calls of honeyeaters and seagulls.
Instead of a snatched breakfast,
    leisurely coffee and rolls in the sunshine.
Instead of the prospect of another day
    focused on a computer screen,
the anticipation of a walk along the beach
    and plunging in the surf.
Instead of prayer on the run,
    a day relaxed with gratitude and praise.

Most loving God, thank you
for the gift of holy-days by the sea
and the renovation that comes
from close contact with your creation.
Through the name of Christ Jesus,
the joy of loving hearts. Amen.

Delight

Like a songbird
basking in spring sunshine,
or an excited child
dancing in the ocean,

help each of us,
O Joy of loving hearts,
to bask with uninhibited ease
in the utter luxury
of your overflowing grace
given to us
in Christ Jesus.

Aussie Things

To Vegemite and fair dinkum mates,
long weekends and Aussie Rules
   add the bonus of your Holy Spirit,
   God of our salvation.
To gum trees and barbecues,
meat pies and flocks of galahs,
to Kakadu and the Melbourne Cup,
the Opera House and bush tucker
   add the bonus of your Holy Spirit,
   God of our salvation.
To Trades Hall and a fair go,
WA wildflowers and Sydney ferries,
to country shows and Melbourne trams,
jackaroos and wild brumbies
   add the bonus of your Holy Spirit,
   God of our salvation.
To cattle stations and life savers,
Anzac Day and campfire damper
   add the bonus of your Holy Spirit,
   God of our salvation.

Things Fixed and Familiar

Lord of all being, friend of the earth, help us to keep our balance in the rush of life. As dazzling changes rush at us like space ships out of the future, we thank you for things that remain fixed and familiar.

We rejoice, loving God,
> in the monolith of Uluru, which lies unperturbed at the red centre of our continent
> in the merriment of kookaburras among the red gums by the Murray River
> in the untiring rhythm of the surf at Bells Beach, Margaret River and Bondi
> in the fish of the Barrier Reef, which do not work to make clothes for themselves yet are beautifully attired.

We rejoice, loving God,
> in the delight of parents watching their child attempt its first faltering steps
> in the tantalising aroma of a favourite meal being cooked in the kitchen
> in the skill of a potter throwing and moulding common clay on the wheel
> in all the hope that is present in marriage vows and the joy of a wedding feast.

We rejoice, loving God,
> in people of courageous faith who tackle the mountains of social injustice
> in the yeast-like word of the gospel and the songs of the people of God
> in the Presence which comes like the wind and inspires like tongues of fire
> in the bread and wine on a common table and the love of a most gracious Host.

Lord of all being, friend of the earth, we praise you for things fixed, familiar and faithful. Through Jesus Christ, the same today, yesterday and forever. Amen.

Celebration

(In the vein of Psalm 148)

Hallelujah!

Joyfully praise God, everywhere and everything!
    Let praise fill the whole cosmos!
Praise God, all races and nations on earth.
    Praise God, all children of the distant stars.

Praise God, sun, moon and the planets.
    Give praise, suns, solar winds and comets.
Praise God, supernovas and spiral nebulae.
    Give praise, black holes and cosmic mysteries.

Praise God, dingo, platypus and wallaroo.
    Give praise, lyrebird, magpie and cockatoo.
Praise God, Huon pine, silky oak and tree fern.
    Give praise, spinifex, mulga and ghost gum.

Praise God, jumbo jet and space shuttle.
    Give praise, pilot, navigator and astronaut.
Praise God, baker, farmer and supermarket.
    Give praise, hospital, bush nurse and flying doctor.

Praise God, all microscopic wonders.
    Give praise, cells, chromosomes and genes.
Praise God, atoms, electrons and quarks.
    Give praise, microchips and microsurgery.

Praise God, chief justice, Koori elder, and prime minister.
    Give praise, painter, musician and comedian.
Praise God, chapel, church and cathedral.
    Give praise, archbishop, priest and pastor.

Let everything praise the goodness of the Creator,
    for God alone can be utterly trusted.
God, our God, is worthy of love and adoration.
    Give praise, everything and everywhere!

Hallelujah!

Laughter

Lord of laughter, open our eyes to see through the
absurdities of this brazen century and to confront
them with good humour rather than faithless despair.

Help us to smile while the wealthy worry
or the politicians strut and dissemble.
Give us the grace to chuckle at technological vainglory
or the self-praise of the entertainment industry.
When ignorance poses as dogmatic scientific wisdom
or the devil's slaves pretend to be angels of light,
enable us to laugh heartily with the faith and daring
that is born of your Easter victory.

Lord of laughter, when we take ourselves too seriously,
laugh at us until we come to our senses.
For your love's sake. Amen.

What Are We?

God, our God,
what are mere humans
    that you think of us,
and the children of earth's dust
    that you visit us?

In the light of wheeling galaxies
    we see the work of your little finger.
In the faith-journey of Abraham and Sarah
    we hear a whisper of your ways.
In the prodigious energy of the atom
    we gain a glimpse of your power.
In the outcry of your prophets
    we hear a hint of your justice.
In a rejected and crucified Jew
    we see the glory of your grace.
On an evening walk to Emmaus
    we meet the love that never ends.

God, our God,
what are mere humans
    that you think of us,
the children of earth's dust
    that you visit us?

Illusion of Absence

Loving God, our elusive yet all-sustaining friend,
    in spite of the negative doubters around us
    we dare to celebrate your glorious presence.

In this postmodern world,
    where the illusion of your absence
    is felt keenly by numerous souls,
    we praise you for your gifts
    that break through to nurture us.

We give thanks
    for the accumulated sanity
    of the holy Scriptures,
    through which you speak to us
    even when our hearts feel cold.

We give thanks
    for the caring communities
    of your holy church,
    where you are present
    with encouragement and healing.

We give thanks
    for those special, holy times
    when for a few seconds or hours
    this world's illusions crack open
    and we glimpse your glory.

Most of all we give thanks
    for the gift of Christ Jesus
    planted disconcertingly in history,
    making plain your saving love
    in the midst of this deceptive era.

Loving God, elusive but faithful friend,
    in spite of our scrappy faith and love
    we dare to celebrate your glorious presence.
    Hallelujah!

Micro Graces

We thank you, loving God, for the effective power of micro graces which are continually at work beneath the macro ostentation of the proud and powerful. We give you thanks that, like yeast and mustard seed, the gifts of faith, hope and love go about their business, quietly achieving contemporary miracles.

We rejoice that our lives are in the hands of a Saviour who notices the fall of a sparrow, numbers the hairs on our heads and calls each of us by name.

Thanks and praise, glory and honour,
be to you today and forever! Amen.

REJOICING
IN CHRIST

REJOICING
IN CHRIST

Still You Come

Lord of love, we praise your coming.

Still you come, irrepressible Christ, to help us discover the word of truth hidden beneath electronic newspapers and synthetic voices, beyond psychedelic lights and soaring rockets. Still you come to us, not as a ghost from the past but as the Spirit of the future, offering us more than we can ask or as yet receive.

We praise your coming, Lord Jesus, and we seek to follow you today better than we did yesterday. To the glory of God and the enrichment of the earth. Amen.

Cut and Polish

Our loving God, your generous Light is here by day, constantly filling all things. Yet most of the people around us do not seem to notice you. They live as if their days are spent in a darkness from which they must snatch fleeting moments of happiness. In their desperation for brief pleasures they trample over one another, without caring for the weak or the maimed.

Saviour God, cut and polish the worship and service of your church until it acts like a prism for your Light. Through our words and deeds make the invisible become visible. Display the rainbow wonder of your Presence, that the lost and the desperate may perceive your beauty and trust the Light in which they live and move and have their being.

God of God, Light of Light, make us a prism for your glory. Through Jesus Christ, our brother and Saviour. Amen.

The Best of Joys

You remain, loving Christ, the joy of our best desiring. You, and you alone, are our light and salvation in a world gone mad worshipping its own contemporary cleverness or lapsing into old recycled religious half-truths and superstitions.

Sure, there were saints and prophets before you, as there are dreams preceding daybreak. Certainly there have been wise ones who came after you, as the moon follows the sun. You alone are the crux of our believing, the ferment in our hoping, the inexhaustible grace of our loving.

You were, are, and will be. Allow us to stay beside you, within you, and always for you, forever and ever. Amen.

Save Us from Experts

Strong Saviour Christ, please continue to save us from the economic experts of this generation.

From experts who approach every question with an open mouth, deliver us.

From those who publish theories as if they were immutable laws, deliver us.

From those who treat market forces as if they were benign agents of social wellbeing, deliver us.

From experts who preach personal greed as a cardinal community virtue, deliver us.

From those who push aside ethical questions with a wave of the latest consumer research, deliver us.

From experts who leave no space for humility, doubts, self-sacrifice and saving grace, deliver us.

Let your words reclaim our attention and allegiance. Remind us that

those who selfishly grab at life will lose it

we cannot serve both God and money

the last shall be first and the first last.

O strong Saviour, confront and discomfort your people. Work relentlessly in us lest we lose touch with the very gospel which we have saluted with our creeds, praised with our hymns and preached from our pulpits.

For your love's sake. Amen.

Healer of Hurts

Come to us, Healer of hurts.
Touch us with your fingers and we shall be saved.

Come to broken hearts and grieving spirits,
to wild anxieties and lost sanity.
Mend us and we shall be whole.

Come to rocky marriages and sore divorces,
to sleepless nights and lost self-confidence.
Mend us and we shall be whole.

Come to dying dreams and painful memories,
to betrayed values and lost opportunities.
Mend us and we shall be whole.

Come to weary wills and dried-up love,
to abandoned hopes and lost faith.
Mend us and we shall be whole.

Healer of hurts, Lord of perfect wholeness,
come to us with your holiness.
Let our ordered lives confess
the beauty of your peace.

Amen.
Amen.

Cosmic Christ

Cosmic Christ, Word of God, in how many forms have you
been born on faraway planets? How many times have you
come to your own creatures but they did not receive you?

How many remarkable parables have you told, how many eyes
have you opened, how many feet have you washed? How often
have you been betrayed and denied, abused and butchered?
How many Easters have changed despair to joy, and how often
have you breathed the Holy Spirit into mortal minds?

O Saviour Christ, Word of God, let transcosmic choirs sing
their gratitude and praise! Let a multitude of loving beings,
with angels and archangels, serve you unceasingly from every
corner of space and time!

Holy, holy, holy, is the Lord of hosts! All things are filled with
your glory! Hosanna in the highest! Amen!

Christ Today

Christ be with me, Christ before me,
Christ be after me, Christ within me,
Christ beneath me, Christ above me,
Christ at my right, Christ at my left,
Christ in the home, Christ on the road,
Christ in the heart of everyone who thinks of me,
Christ in the mouth of everyone who speaks with me,
Christ in every eye that sees me,
Christ in every ear that listens to me.

St Patrick (AD 385–461)

O My Jesus!

O my Christ Jesus!
Without you and your gift
of faith in the living God
my life would be nothing
but a dogged decency,
lived with many difficulties
among burgeoning technology
and sustained by an angry defiance
flung against the deep darkness
of monstrous despair.

O my Christ Jesus,
thank you for being you
and thoroughly saving me
from darkness and dread.
Amen.

The Saving Love

Lord Jesus, you stretched out your arms of love on the hard
wood of the cross, that all people might come within the reach
of your saving embrace. Clothe us in your Spirit, that we,
stretching out our hands in loving service for others, may bring
those who do not know you to an awareness and love of you;
who with the Father and the Holy Spirit live and reign, one God
forever. Amen.

C H Brent (1862–1929)

Take Joy

Take joy, lovely Lord,
in all who ask, seek,
knock, find and enter
into your new world.

Take joy, lovely Lord,
wherever two or three
are gathered together
in your name.

Take joy, lovely Lord,
when your followers
seek not to be served
but to serve.

Take joy, lovely Lord,
when enemies are loved,
the persecuted are prayed for
and wrongs are forgiven.

Take joy, lovely Lord,
wherever great love
proves that many sins
are indeed forgiven.

Take joy, lovely Lord,
with those who are taught
by the birds of the bush
and the wildflowers.

Take joy, lovely Lord,
in the unpretentious folk
who give parties for those who are poor,
crippled, lame and blind.

Take joy, lovely Lord,
with those who find joy
in one lost sinner
who turns to God.

Take joy, lovely Lord,
wherever eyes are opened
in the breaking of bread
with a Stranger.

Take joy, lovely Lord,
in all who are immersed
in your remarkable news
and soaked in love.

Healer

Healer
of ragged hopes
and tattered ideals,

Nurse
of faint faith
and fractured creeds,

Physician
of listless lives
and limping love,

at evening,
before the sun is set,
lay your hands on us.

Touch Our Eyes

What a strange mixture we are, most patient God. Insatiable in
our searching, bold with our theories, surrounded with
electronic enchantments, yet creatures of boundless blindness
when it comes to the things that ultimately matter.

Send to us that holy Man who made a salve from clay and
touched the eyes of the blind. May he touch us and restore to
us a sane view of life. Let us see ourselves as beings made for
worship, fellowship, justice and love. Enable us to treasure our
friends and pray for our enemies, serve our neighbours and
seek first the kingdom of God and its righteousness.

Touch our eyes that we may become what we really are.
Through Christ Jesus our Lord. Amen.

Christ in the Third Millennium

We delight, most loving God, in the continuing influence of Christ Jesus in this third millennium.

Wonderful is the God and Father of our Lord Jesus, who has blessed us with every spiritual blessing in Christ.

In every stimulating advance we make, he is there, well ahead of us, asking us to go on in faith.

What eye has not seen, or ear heard, or the mind conceived God has in store for those who love him.

Where we take a wrong turn and end up in a maze of contemporary doubts and anxieties, Christ is there to lead us through.

You have not chosen me. I have chosen you. By grace you are saved, through faith; not by your efforts but as a gift of God.

If we become disheartened by the ability of evil to adopt new forms and corrupt new achievements, he speaks with us.

I will not leave you all alone; I will come to you. Cheer up, for I have overcome the evil of this world.

When we are disgusted with our own folly and sin, in the name of God Christ forgives us and lifts us up.

I did not come to condemn but to save. Daughter, son, your sins are forgiven you. Go in peace.

Whenever we are confused by the tough ethical decisions to be made by citizens of this twenty-first century, Christ is with us.

Seek first the kingdom of God and its righteousness, and all that you need will be given to you. Love one another as I have loved you.

We delight, most loving God, in all that Christ once was, is now, and ever will be.

Neither life nor death, things present nor things to come, will be able to separate us from the love of God in Christ Jesus our Lord.

(This may be followed by a sung doxology.)

I Believe

Jesus Christ, brother of light,
I believe.

I believe
that in the beginning was the Promise,
and the Promise was with God,
and the Promise was God.

I believe
in the infinite, nurturing creativity of God,
in the incarnate, crucified humility of God,
in the intimate, inspiring liberality of God.

Jesus Christ, brother of light,
I believe.

Source of Glory

Jesus, joy of the heart's desiring,
   work your transforming skills
   in and through us.
Make us humble without realising it,
   wise without showing it,
   loving without calculating it
   and good without knowing it,
that your grace may speak
   through us but not of us
and others may come to seek
   the Source of the glory
   which they have fleetingly
   glimpsed in our common being.
For your name's sake. Amen.

C H Brent (1862–1929)

To the God We Fear

Eternal God, we fear you yet we adore you!

We fear a love so daring and puzzling that you permit evil and suffering to abound in your universe.

We adore a love so determined and costly that you bore in a human body the full agony of this world.

With Job we shout out our protest. With John we say there is no greater love than this.

Eternal God, the ever-present victim and victor, take both our fear and our faith and let them serve you today and declare your glory forever. Through Jesus Christ our Lord. Amen.

MOVING WITH THE CHURCH

MOVING WITH THE CHURCH

What of the Church?

God of each unexpected breakthrough, of quantum surprises and faithful revisitings, where does the church fit into your plans?

We cannot see where you are taking us or what the shape of the church will be. Things we have treasured appear to be dying, while trends that make us anxious seem to be emerging. At times we experience loss, grief and anger, yet on other occasions we feel excitement and hope.

Remind us of the paradox of your strength in Christ Jesus: that people who hoard their life will lose it, yet those who lose it for the gospel's sake will find it.

Replace our worrying with a firmer faith, and give us the kind of wisdom that knows the right time in which to bring out from the storehouse of the church's story things that are old or things that are brand new.

Let us journey boldly where the timid dare not tread. Let us meet gladly at that table where generations have been fed.

For the sake of your new world and the glory that was, is now, and is to come. In Christ's name. Amen.

Program Us

God our Saviour, as we meet together on the first day of the week, reprogram us with your wisdom. Give us the capacity to work boldly and humbly with the risks and opportunities which confront us, knowing that nothing is ahead of your foresight nor outside of your strength. Through Jesus Christ our brother and Lord. Amen.

The Church and Change

Most patient and loving God, we confess that your church is not good at coping with change.

We anxiously cling to large buildings until the last few survivors are too weary to carry on. We are bewildered by freelance Christians who do not have our dogged loyalty to a denomination. We take offence at those we fear are shifting the ethical goal posts. We complain about changes in church music or liturgy and grumble at innovations in church organisation or outreach.

Defend us, merciful God, against bouts of nostalgic pig-headedness. We are in danger of looking for you in the past but missing your vibrant Spirit in the present and the future. Come to our aid, we pray.

Give your church in these changing times the liberty
    to treasure its heritage without sentimentalising it,
    to seize contemporary opportunity without idolising it,
    to plan for the future without glamorising it.
By your Christ free us, with your Spirit lead us, in your eternal love keep us, until the church becomes more yours than ours, a body fit to declare your glory. Through Jesus Christ our Saviour. Amen.

Come Again, Foot-washer

God, how selfish and competitive
    is this twenty-first century!
And how divided and self-serving
    are the branches of the church!

May he whose name is Foot-washer,
    Son of Common Man,
    Wounded Healer,
    Jesus-Saviour,
    Son of True God,
come again with his unique glory
    to call, heal and gather
    his scattered flock
    into one harmonious outpouring
    of love and service.
For your love's sake. Amen.

New Songs

(In the vein of Psalm 149)

Sing songs of a new age to God,
    sing praises when you gather together!
Let the church celebrate its Creator,
    let the body rejoice in its Head!
Make music with guitar and keyboard,
    tap your feet in the rhythm of praise!
For God delights in today's faithful,
    decorating you with grace upon grace.
Get high on the joy of gratitude,
    sing from church pew or armchair at home!

Let praises fill up your throats!
    Let the Word be a laser in your hands
to bring judgment on nations
    and justice to all races,
to put dictators under arrest
    and bring war criminals to court.
To let the Word do the judging—
    this is glory to believers.

New Age Delusions

Loving God, in these days when occult superstitions, New Age delusions and fringe-church excesses capture the headlines, give us quiet minds and strong wills. Keep us fixed and final in the saving activity of our Lord Jesus Christ.

Nurture in us the genuine humility of faith. Help us to see that what ultimately matters is
    not our search for you but your search for us
    not our knowledge of you but your knowledge of us
    not our hold on you but your hold on us
    not our spiritual techniques but your saving grace
    not our love of you but your love of us.

In the midst of popular new religious fashions and reinvented old heresies, keep us 'as cunning as serpents and as harmless as doves'. Through the grace of our Lord Jesus Christ, the love of God, and the fellowship of the Holy Spirit. Amen.

A Litany for the Times

(Inspired by Ecclesiastes 3:1–7 and Colossians 3:12–17)

Leader: Lord of millennia, Redeemer of each moment, Head of the church, we thank you that there are appropriate seasons and opportune times for everything under the sun.
People: *In whatever we do, let it be done with thanks, in the name of our Lord Jesus.*
Leader: There is a time for birth and a time for death,
    a time for sowing, a time for reaping,
    a time to prune back the old, a time to graft in the new,
    a time to demolish and a time to rebuild.
People: *Let the peace of Christ rule in our hearts, in whom we are called to be one body.*
Leader: A time to repent, a time to celebrate,
    a time to mourn, a time to dance,
    a time to throw away, a time to collect,
    a time to hug, a time to stand alone.
People: *Let the word of Christ live richly in us, that we may sing psalms, hymns and gospel songs in thanksgiving.*
Leader: A time to search, a time to lose oneself,
    a time to hold tight, a time to throw away,
    a time to tear apart, a time to stitch up,
    a time to be quiet, a time to speak out.
People: *Above all else, let us be clothed with love that binds everything together in complete harmony, to the glory of God. Amen.*

Unanimous Goodness

O God the Father, origin of divinity, good that is beyond all good, lovely beyond all that is lovely, in you there is calmness, peace and harmony. End the arguments that divide us from each other, and bring us back to a unity of love, which will bear some likeness to your divine nature. As you oversee all things, bring us to a unanimous goodness, that through the embrace of love and in the ties of affection we may be spiritually one. Through the grace, the mercy, and the tenderness of your Son, Jesus Christ. Amen.

Dionysius Telmaharensis (d AD 845)

The Table

Lord
of simplicity,
cement the legs of your table
into the rock floor
of my little house of faith;

then,
should the bailiffs
of contemporary doubt
arrive at my door
with their bullying ways
to dispossess me
of my religious furniture
and cushioned comforts,

there
will remain
that one altar of love,
where I may place
a roll of bread
and cup of wine,

and
I will know that
all is well,
and all manner of things
will be well.

Closing Churches

Give your people the will, loving God, to close down some
churches with the same faith and vision with which we open
them. Let us give thanks for all precious memories, but do not
permit us to live in them. Inspire us to move on gratefully and
graciously, to worship and witness in new places and in new
ways. And may the God of hope fill us with all joy and peace
in believing. Amen.

Returning to Perfection

God of unchanging power and eternal light, look generously at your whole church, that wonderful and sacred mystery, and carry out the work of our salvation. Let the whole world feel and see that things which were cast down are being raised up, and things which had grown old are being made young, and all things are returning to perfection. Through Jesus Christ our Lord. Amen.

Gelasian Sacramentary (c AD 495)

An Odd Mob

Loving God, we are an odd mob. We thank you for the widely different types of people and expressions of faith which constitute the membership of your church in this century.

We give thanks for those who appear born to express faith through rigid creeds and behaviour.

We give thanks for others who seem destined to follow Christ among innumerable questions and doubts.

We give thanks for members whose faith appears to be a profound childlike simplicity, unhurried and unworried.

We give thanks for those who seem unable to find one satisfying word with which to describe you, yet whose faith is constantly renewed by a wordless awe in the presence of unnameable Love.

Lover of diversity, God of all souls, continue to give us the grace to treasure each other with all our oddness and to use these differences as we minister to the diversity of people who share this twenty-first century with us.

To your praise and glory. Amen.

Special Christians

We say thanks, generous God, for those special Christians who
are much tougher, and yet more tender, than we are:

who keep their balance in the midst of changes that cause us
to waver this way and that

whose love of justice, truth and mercy inspires them to
deeds exceeding what is expected

who never withdraw from the misery and cries of their
fellow human beings

whose faith looks for no escape from sticky situations of
misunderstanding or hostility

who embrace awkward and hard-to-love people without
stiffness or reservation

who forgive their enemies and go the second mile with no
hint of self-congratulation

whose sense of humour leads them to laugh while we
whinge and lick our wounds

whose everyday love and hope counterbalance the avarice
and cynicism of society.

God of all courageous and debonair souls, if we cannot
emulate their character and deeds, may we at least have the
grace to support them and pray for them. Through Christ
Jesus, the strongest and most grace-full of them all. Amen.

Worry and the Church

Leader: We have been stupid again, God. We have let our faith
be corroded by the worries of the world.

People: *We are more aware of fear than hope, more familiar
with anxiety than serenity.*

Leader: We confess that this acidic unfaith even eats away at
our church committees, councils and worship.

People: *We worry, worry, worry about falling numbers and our
declining influence in society.*

Leader: We even worry about the possibility of the church
becoming extinct.

People: *Then we become weary and irritable with one another.*

Lord, have mercy.   *Lord, have mercy.*

Christ, have mercy.   *Christ, have mercy.*

Lord, have mercy.   *Lord, have mercy.*

Leader: Most loving and ever-faithful God, return us to the sanity of faith. Help us to let go of our worrying habits and stand empty in the presence of your abundant grace.

People: *Remind us that the church is yours, not ours. In its strength or in its weakness, keep us faithful to the gospel of Christ and alert to your Spirit's pulse.*

Leader: If it is your will that aspects of the church that we have loved must die, let us embrace death gracefully.

People: *If it is your plan that a new church should be born, let us suffer the travail gratefully.*

Leader: Fill us with courage, a sense of humour and a quiet mind.

People: *For yours is the kingdom, power and glory of irrepressible love, today, tomorrow and forever. Amen.*

A Third-millennium Church

Loving God, great is your resourcefulness! Your new ideas are past numbering! Your unexpected mercies break through all barriers!

We thank you that the church is your creation, not ours. Help us to cooperate with your Spirit in this new age, so that we may be and do whatever is best in this world for which Christ Jesus died.

Save us from the twin dangers of either pathetically clinging to the past or foolishly craving novelties. Shape us with the gospel that we may be both conservative and radical, liberal and narrow, imaginative and prudent.

By the grace of Christ Jesus, enable us to be enthusiastic in prayer, eager in Bible study, debonair in witness, cheerful in service, and high-spirited in worship.

Should there be times of outward shrinking of your church, open our eyes to see the new horizons where your rejuvenating Holy Spirit is at work in power.

In the name of the Father, the Son and the Holy Spirit. Amen.

ADORING THE MYSTERY

ADORING
THE MYSTERY

You See through Me

(From Psalm 139)

Loving God, you see through me and know me.
　　Whether I rush or rest, you are with me.
When I wander, you seek me out;
　　you always recognise what I am up to.
Before I can turn thoughts into words,
　　you understand my deepest longings.

Where could I ever lose touch with you?
　　Where could I escape your presence?
If I rocket through the skies of outer space,
　　or meet other children of the stars,
you will be waiting for me out there,
　　still loving me without limit.
If everything on earth goes wrong
　　and the world becomes sheer hell,
even then your hand will lead me,
　　your right hand will tightly hold me.
If I slip into the darkness of depression,
　　each day as gloomy as deep night,
you are the torch at my side,
　　the radiance at the end of the tunnel.

O God, your thoughts for me are precious.
　　Their total defies computation,
they outnumber the sand and the stars,
　　yet at the end there is much more.
See through me and test my feelings,
　　sift me and sample my thoughts,
uncover anything that is infected
　　and lead me on the boundless journey.
Amen.

You Are

You are the Surprise from whom all discoveries grow,
    the Delight of whom each victory sings,
    the Joy to whom all lasting pleasures flow,
    the Search out of whom all science springs,
    the Truth who surfaces when all seems lost,
    the Love who will not count the cost.
Creating God, high above our understanding,
    we worship your mystery!
Redeeming God, deep beyond our deserving,
    we worship your mystery!
Inspiring God, near beyond our knowing,
    we worship your mystery!
Amen! And again we say Amen!

A Creed: Lord of the Stars

We believe!
We believe in you, one God, maker of heaven and earth.

We believe you have not left yourself without witness
    among the stars.
In our galaxy, within the immense majesty of the Milky Way,
    you are ever present.
Outside our galaxy, through the wonders of worlds unknown,
    you are at work.

We believe that wherever other creatures might live, think and
    feel,
    you have shown and commanded love.
Whenever beings have rebelled and fallen into damnation,
    you have come to them as Saviour.
There is no corner of any distant planet, no child of the stars,
    outside your infinite providence.

O great Shepherd of the stars, who calls each by name, we
rejoice in your ever-presence. You have not forgotten the small
planet which we call home but have crowned it with glory and
honour by coming to us in your true Son, Christ Jesus. Holy,
holy, holy are you! Heaven and earth are full of your glory!

Lord God, maker of heaven and earth, we believe!

Beyond Noisy Words

You, who fill heaven and earth, always busy, always quiet, who are present everywhere and everywhere are fully present; you who are not absent when far away, who with your whole being fill yet go beyond all things; you who teach the hearts of the faithful without the din of words, teach us, we pray. Through Jesus Christ our Lord. Amen.

St Augustine of Hippo (AD 354–430)

You Are God!

God, you are God! The Splendour we cannot imagine, the Wisdom we cannot contain, the Power we cannot manipulate, the Love we cannot buy.

God, you are God! The Source of our purest longings, the Grace that redeems our failings.
God, you are God! The faithful Lover of humanity, the Friend of sinners.
God, you are God! The crucified one bruised for our iniquities, the Word that wakes the dead.

God, you are God! And we, a few of those creatures who have found a little faith and love, will worship and serve you all our days. In the name of the Father, Son and Holy Spirit. Amen.

Encounters of a Fourth Kind?

Lord of life, what an outburst of wonder there will be on earth if one day we make contact with other beings from among the starry skies. Yet how much more wonder-full it is that we already have been given contact with the very Creator of the cosmos! We are a visited planet: hallelujah!

O Wonder beyond wonders! O Joy beyond joys! Exhilaration and praise, exultation and glory, love and yearning adoration belong to you from every place on planet Earth! Hallelujah! Amen!

Hints of God

You God, you who are the Bread that sustains our being and
the Light that opens our eyes, we recognise some of your
providential ways.

You give the warmth that radiates from a stone wall after an
hour in the winter sunshine.
You come with the spinifex pigeons, picking among the red
sand for the crumbs of our camp breakfast.
You whisper in the composers, whose symphonies rise far
above their own experience.
You fill the small stream, rippling for a brief season between
extensive droughts.
You strengthen the young joeys, exploring the world with
bounding enthusiasm.
You speak from the handicapped person, selling papers by the
railway station.
You sing with the lone blackbird, sending a defiant song into a
bitter August dawn.
You fill the outback waterhole, fed by subterranean streams
from rains that fell long ago.
You visit us with the wind in desert sheoaks, singing through
long, lonely nights.
You confront us in the child, arguing about the fairness of the
parable of the workers in the vineyard.
You treasure the surviving grapevines that survive around the
ruins of a pioneer's stone cottage.
You meet us in the gnarled arthritic fingers serving us bread in
the house of prayer.

O God, you who are holy humility and mundane immediacy,
we recognise some of your ways. Praise and glory, honour and
love, joy and celebration belong to you in all the earth!
Through Jesus Christ our Lord. Amen.

Open Our Eyes

*Lord, we pray that you will open our eyes to behold the heaven
that lies about us, wherein they walk who, being born of the
new life, serve you with the clearer vision and the greater joy.
Amen.*

R L Stevenson (1850–94)

To a Much-ignored God

Much-ignored God, pity our self-important attempts to live without reference to you. Bring us to our senses.

We are lost, even in our own homes, until you call our names. We are deceived until your truth breaks through all counterfeits. We are uptight with self-justifications until your grace relaxes us. We are at war with ourselves until you bring a peace which
    outstrips all self-help therapies.
Without you, we spend ourselves in counterproductive activity, bereft of adequate purpose and devoid of lasting value. With you, we participate in the wondrous patterns and beauties of infinite purposefulness.

Come to us, then, much-ignored God. Come to us and mesh our brash littleness with your graceful immensity. Through Jesus Christ our Lord. Amen.

Science and Knowledge

Sooner or later, O God, our adventurous race may one day explore everything which is within your universe. We may uncover the last secret of our remarkable brains and chart the final stars of outer space.

But you we cannot explore or measure: no maps, no theories, no mathematical formulae, no microscopic or telescopic photos. We see nothing of your mystery unless you choose to reveal it. We have no knowledge of you unless you chose to teach us.

Humbly and gratefully we give thanks for the revelation that you have given, for the little you have chosen to teach us. Most of all, we thank you for Jesus of Nazareth, who is the mirror image of your grace and truth. We hold on to him with love and adoration. Through him we offer you ourselves, with the elementary science we now possess and all the staggering discoveries that are to come. To you all thanks, praise and glory belong. Through Jesus Christ. Amen.

The Mystery

Awesome Cosmic-Creator, how inadequately we understand you!
Wonderful Brother-Redeemer, how glibly we speak of you!
Pervasive Friend-Spirit, how shallowly we inhale you!

Holy, holy, holy, is the Lord of hosts! All things are filled with your inexplicable glory!

Our loftiest creeds chart only a corner of your kingdom. Our noblest deeds explore only the fringes of your ways. All the books in all the theological libraries of the world are like the chatter of little children who have paddled in the shallows of the ocean.

Yet we celebrate all we can know of you through the gift of Christ Jesus. He makes the difference between faith and fear, hope and despair, love and apathy, joy and angst, madness and praise. Through him we offer you the best of our praise and the holiest of our deeds. Amen.

Why?

Why do you hide yourself so effectively, God? Why do you make faith such a gamble? Why can't you show yourself unambiguously, so that each person may make up their mind whether to be a lover or a rebel?

As things are, all the boundaries are blurred. There are numerous choice souls in the community who live their whole life in the shadowland between faith and disbelief. Some of the finest loyal people in your church go through dark times when they wonder if they are following an illusion. Even your wonderful saints have periods of black emptiness.

Truly, you are a frustrating God! If it were not for my interminable hunger that has tasted the bread from Jesus of Nazareth, I would have given you up long ago!

First Love

Dear love
   first love
   last love
all-loving love

Pure joy
   at the nucleus of today
   waiting to be
received

Cup overflowing
   the best wine
   that is kept
until the last

Pristine love
   priceless pearl
   yet given away
   and shared
by beggars

Time-free love
   beginning
   at the end
redeeming

Love saying
   'you are saved
   come with me
   be what you are
my beloved'

Dear Love
   it is you
   we love
and adore

Sweet Bargain

O my God, let me walk in the way of that love which does not know how to be selfish. Let me love you just for yourself, and nothing else but in you and for you. Let me love nothing instead of you. To give all for love is a most sweet bargain. Let your love work in me and by me, and let me love you as you would want to be loved. Amen.

Gertrude More (1606–33)

G.O.D

God. G.o.d. These three letters with which we name you are a pathetic inadequacy.

How can one word carry the message of the origin of that massive glory, the fringes of which astronomers and space probes are encountering within the majesty of the cosmos?

How can this one word convey, or even hint at, the source of the intricate glory which geneticists are unravelling within all living things?

How can one three-letter word serve to point to the secret of the glory which medical science is exploring within the human brain and philosophers ponder within the phenomenon of self-consciousness?

How shall we, who are of the church, use this frail word 'God' to declare the incomparable glory of saving, healing love which we still find confronting us in Christ Jesus?

O Source and Goal of our being, Joy and Light of our aspiring, all our words are too inadequate to even hint at your adequacy! Help us to back up our use of the word 'God' with such integrity, love, humility and a sense of awe that others may catch a glimpse of the wonder that has touched and redeemed us and of the Spirit who, incognito, is at work within them.

Through Jesus Christ, our brother and Lord. Amen.

The Trinity

You, eternal Trinity, are a deep sea, into which the more I enter the more I find, and the more I find the more I seek. The soul cannot be satiated in your abyss, for she continually hungers after you, the eternal Trinity, desiring to see you with the light of light. As the tongue desires springs of running water, so my soul desires to leave this dark body to see you in truth. O abyss, O eternal Godhead, O sea profound, what more could you give me other than yourself? Amen.

St Catherine of Sienna (1347–80)

The Intimate Absence

You
   who are the active stillness,
the outer rim
yet inner hub
   of all that is
   or ever will be.

You,
   the intimate absence,
the presence we know,
yet whose fullness
   flows far outside
   our understanding.

You,
   the Christmas extravagance,
the love self-limited
within one human life,
   yet embracing millions
   and transcending stars.

You,
   who are the Easter folly,
the God who dies alone,
yet whose abundant life
   neither tomb nor hell confines
   nor even heaven contains.

Glory in the highest!

Above Electronic Babel

May the silence of the Most High
    flow around us and within us.
Above the electronic babel of this new era
    may the Holy Silence fall upon us.
May the silence of the Most High
    inform and teach us.
May the silence of the Most High
    calm and heal us.
May the silence of the Most High
    lead us to the incarnate Word,
    fill us with wisdom and courage,
and direct our feet in the way of peace.

LOVING ONE ANOTHER

LOVING
ONE ANOTHER

Love and the Global Village

God of Christ Jesus, the task of loving every neighbour as we love ourselves has become too big for us. The world is now too small, its population too large, the burden of its evil and misery too enormous.

We dare not pray with earlier generations for 'such kindness of heart that we may sympathise with every affliction and feel for every misfortune, as if it were our own'.* To do so would be to fail you. Under its load we would become broken in spirit and body, numbered among the world's victims rather than its healers.

Therefore we pray to you for common sense. Let each of us be ready to do what can reasonably be done, add a little more by your grace, and then leave the rest to you and your other servants.

And God have mercy on us all. Amen.

Nakatenus, 17th-century priest

For World Peace

Bless, O God, all who dedicate their powers today to the making of peace in the world. Bless all who give their training and experience to feed and clothe and house the destitute. Bless all who lend their energies and skills to teach impoverished people to till, water and harvest their land. And give us all a lively concern for the underprivileged, and show us practical ways for helping. For Christ's sake. Amen.

Rita Snowden (20th century)

Wars and Rumours of Wars

Wouldn't you think, Lord, that we could have applied the
wonders of our advanced science and brilliant technology to
producing peace on earth and goodwill among the nations?
Wouldn't you expect that with the libraries of civilisation on
the internet we would have now learnt how to get on with one
another?

Yet here we are, competitive and callous, divided and divorced,
blinded by the tribal politics, inventing new weapons of war,
fearing the truth, avoiding the love which is true life.

O Saviour Christ, enter our being with a word sharper than a
sword, prune the deep roots of our wanting and willing,
nurture us with your free grace which from a cross reconciles
all things.

Make us advanced in the things of the Spirit until our hearts
are joined in a common purpose and our deeds declare your
glory. Amen.

Injustice and Suffering

God of all, the clamour of this world's injustice and suffering is
too much with us. Its cries hurt our ears, its sad faces haunt
our eyes. From television and telephone, mailbox and fax, it
begs for our charity.

God, we cannot cope with it all! The weight of it pushes us
down into laborious, guilt-driven activity or towards a self-
protective indifference.

Saviour God, deliver us from trying to be a messiah or from
evading our responsibilities. From among the multiplicity of
righteous works that need to be done, help us to recognise the
few that we can do and to do them well. Give us the humility
and the sanity to leave the total scene to you and those others
of your servants whom you enlist.

By your unlimited love and untimed patience, bring nearer that
day when weeping will turn to laughter and fear to dancing,
when 'justice shall roll down like waterfalls and righteousness
like an ever-flowing stream'.

For your love's sake. Amen.

The Disadvantaged

God of love, have mercy on the world of human affairs, where the gap between the advantaged and disadvantaged seems to be ever widening.

We pray for all victims of this injustice:
for the sick and the maimed who cannot afford the latest in medical technology;
for the hungry millions who have been denied the benefits of genetically improved grains, fruits and meats;
for indigenous minorities, whose health and education prospects lag far behind those of the general population;
for the unemployed, who have been cast aside by the electronic revolution in industry and commerce;
for the second and third generation of refugees who are still living in camps that were set up in the previous century;
for small nations, who are being exploited or shut out of markets by the strong and aggressive;
for the poor, who cannot afford to pay the cost of obtaining justice in courts of law.

God of justice and mercy, keep your church faithful and compassionate. Do not permit us to become so concerned with our own weaknesses that we neglect to love our neighbour as Christ Jesus has loved us. In his name we pray. Amen.

Divorced

Loving God, our prayers reach out to the newly divorced. Once they made their vows before you, radiant with love and hope, convinced they had found a soul mate for life.

Today they are a mixture of grief and relief, aching from a raw wound in their being, uncertain of their own wisdom, distrustful of others, anxious about the future.

Saviour-Friend, with the tendrils of your Spirit reach into the secret places of the deepest hurt. Cleanse the wounds and begin the process of healing. Restore their broken self-confidence and grant them the invaluable gift of your peace.

In the days ahead, be to them the friend whose love never wearies and the Lord who redeems the unhappy years.

For your love's sake. Amen.

The Nervously Ill

Lord of great compassion, we pray you for those who are
nervously ill and too weak or anxious to lift themselves above
the fear and sadness that threaten to overwhelm them. Do you
yourself, Lord, lift them up and deliver them, as you delivered
your disciples in the storm at sea, strengthening their faith and
banishing their fear. Turning to you, may they find you, and
finding you may they find also all you have laid up for them
within the fortress of your love. Amen.

Elizabeth Goudge (1900–84)

The Mercy of Justice

Where are things heading, God of wisdom?
Unless you are a God of justice and judgment,
    the future of this arrogant world is dismal.
Unless you are a God of grace and mercy,
    our place in your future is hopeless.

With the anger of a temple cleansing,
    overthrow greed and scatter our indifference.
With the suffering of your crucified Son,
    forgive our sins and heal our diseases.
With the mercy of justice and the justice
    of your unique mercy, lead us on towards
    the consummation of your kingdom.

You alone are our help and hope.
You alone are our health and happiness.
Through Jesus Christ our Saviour. Amen.

Poverty and Hunger

Make us worthy, Lord, to serve our fellows throughout the world
who live and die in poverty and hunger. Give them, through our
hands, this day their daily bread. And by our understanding
love, give joy and peace. Amen.

Mother Teresa of Calcutta (1910–97)

For Our City

O God, grant us a new vision for our city, as fair as she might be:

> *a city of justice, where none shall prey on others;*

> *a city of plenty, where vice and poverty shall not fester;*

> *a city of brotherhood, where success shall be founded on service;*

> *a city of peace, where order shall not rest on force but on love for all.*

Hear the prayer of all our hearts as we each pledge our time, strength and thought to speed the coming day of beauty and righteousness. Amen.

W Rauschenbusch (1861–1918)

Seizing the Opportunity

God of all peoples and all times, inspire us to seize the opportunities of this century with faith, hope and love:

to apply the best scientific skills to reverse the degradation of land and stream, sea and air;
to shape political parties that without fear or favour will govern with justice and compassion;
to make the best medical practice and hospital care accessible to all people;
to ensure that space exploration is for the common good and not for the power or greed of a few;
to use fax, internet and videophone to foster peace on earth and goodwill among all people;
to make certain that our courts and true justice are available to the least and last citizen among us;
to apply genetic engineering to eliminate malnutrition and hunger rather than increase the profits of multinationals;
to follow the Spirit as it rebuilds the church as one family in worship, fellowship and service.

For these challenges and many more, give us the will to turn our prayers into programs and actions and, where needful, into loving self-sacrifice. Through Jesus Christ our Lord. Amen.

The Poor

As you once said, Lord Jesus, the poor are always with us.
Overseas and in our land, in crowded refugee camps and
sleeping on our city streets. The poor. Your much-loved poor.

Some are poor by choice, some by their foolishness, some by
calamity, and many because of the greed of the rich and the
indifference of the comfortable.

Christ, have mercy on us all. Give us the political will and
know-how to lessen the injustices that perpetuate poverty.
Bless the efforts of the religious and secular agencies that reach
out with disciplined compassion. Prompt each of us to do
whatever seems possible and then to prayerfully consider what
more can be done.

In the meantime, while we are now praying, touch the lives of
your children who are in poverty with blessings which the rich
cannot know. For your love's sake. Amen.

For Balanced Lives

God of holiness, save us from everything that distracts or
debases our longing for truth, beauty and goodness.
God of wholeness, restore a balance to our pressured, lopsided
lives.

May eyes trained for video screens and traffic lights have time
to delight in pygmy possums and banksia blossoms.
May ears force-fed with sensational news and loud music find
pleasure in the rippling of creeks and the songs of blue wrens.
May noses flooded with exhaust and industrial fumes savour
again the scent of wild boronia or a salty sea breeze.
May hands addicted to the touch of credit cards and ATMs
find release in the clasp of a child or the passing of the peace.
May minds bruised with information overload be open to the
gospel parables and the plight of the needy.
May appetites pampered with wines or sated with junk food
be renewed by the bread of life and the cup of salvation.

God of holiness, God of wholeness, through the simple gifts of
your creation restore our balance, and through the grace of
Christ Jesus heal us all. For your name's sake. Amen.

Be with Us: A Litany

You, wonderful God, whose glory the heavens declare
and whose handiwork the whole earth sees,
be with astronomers and astronauts,
artists, photographers and bushwalkers.
You, whose Spirit brooded over the face of the earth
and brought breath to all that lives and grows,
be with health workers who control viruses and bacteria
or engineer genes and chromosomes.
You, for whom truth is not mere facts and figures
but relationship and the gift of eternal love,
be with those whose science has left them empty
or whose technology has become a slavery.
You, who give us faith that leads to many doubts
and deep doubts that lead to a larger faith,
be with all agnostics and those who despair
and all the pure of heart who hunger for you.
You, who have created us for fulfilment and joy
and do not rest while one lost person is in misery,
be with those who are lost in amusement arcades
or imprisoned by poker machines and casinos.
You, who cherish us as your very own family,
even if mother and father forsake us,
be with abused children and street kids,
social workers, magistrates and foster parents.
You, who when thick darkness covered humanity,
leapt into the night bringing light and joy,
be with night-shift workers and police,
evangelists, counsellors and pastors.
You, whose first-born, perfect Child
covered our sins and bore our griefs,
be with mothers and midwives,
the falsely accused and sorely abused.
You, who banish fears and bring a new dawn,
who swallow up death in victory,
be with those who risk their lives for others
and all who today face death alone.
You, who know our needs before we utter them
and do far more than we can ask or imagine,
be with us as we offer these prayers
and with all who have forgotten how to pray.
Through Jesus Christ, our brother and Saviour.
Amen and Amen!

For the New Kingdom

God, the Father of all, you have lovingly made the peoples of the world to be one family. Help those of different races and religions to love, understand and accept one another. Take away all hatred, jealousy and prejudice, so that all may work together for the coming of your kingdom of righteousness and peace; through Jesus Christ our Lord. Amen.

Evelyn Underhill (1875–1941)

The Opposition

God of all times and all people, teach us to listen to the things you have to say and to notice the good things you are doing through people who seem to oppose us.

Open our eyes to what you are doing through the political parties for whom we will never vote.
Open our ears to the word you speak through those Christians whose theology and worship appear to be at odds with much of the faith which we hold.
Open our minds to the light you may have to shed through religions which are not of the Christian fold.
Open our consciences to the new challenges with which you confront us through those whose sincere moral convictions startle or offend us.

Spirit of living truth, give us generous hearts and discerning minds, that we may travel through the maze of this world's opinions with compassion for our enemies and a passion to love you with all our heart, soul, mind and strength. Through Jesus Christ our Saviour. Amen.

Growing Old

Jesus, who never grew old, it is not easy for any of us to face old age. It is fine to be young, attractive, strong. Old age reminds us of weakness and dependence on others. But to be your disciple means accepting weakness and interdependence. Because of you we can rejoice in weakness in ourselves and be tender to it in others.

Monica Furlong (b 1930)

I Shall Not Want

God, of your goodness, give me yourself, for you are sufficient for me. I cannot properly ask anything less, to be worthy of you. If I were to ask less, I would always be in want. In you alone do I have all.

Lady Julian of Norwich (AD 1342–1417)

A Blessing

Deep peace of the running wave be yours.

Deep peace of the flowing air be yours.

Deep peace of the quiet earth be yours.

Deep peace of the shining stars be yours.

The deep, deep peace of the Son of peace be yours.

From a Celtic benediction

FOLLOWING
EACH DAY

FOLLOWING
EACH DAY

Not by Any Chance

Save us, redeeming God, from the glitz and despair of the contemporary casino culture of our nation.

We rejoice in the unique place each one of us holds in your purposes. We thank you that we have not haphazardly appeared on earth like numbers on lotto balls but at the right place at the right time in your providence. Before we were born you planned for us. From childhood to old age you cherish and guide us. At the far end of the valley of the shadow of death you prepare a place for us. In this very moment, loving Friend, you call us to share in your love for the world.

O God of complex providence and inexhaustible love, let us fulfil the purposes for which we were born. Through Jesus Christ our Saviour. Amen.

The Hubble Telescope

We thank you, loving Creator, for the vision, energy and brilliant technology which set the Hubble telescope and its successors in orbit. As the human mind probes further than ever before, more of the colossal grandeur of creation is revealed, and we become aware of the magnitude of what still lies out of our reach. Do not let our discoveries diminish our faith but enlarge it. Lead us to a greater awe and wonder, to a worship which is enriched by the contemplation of the work of your fingers, and a gratitude that is even more amazed by the holy incarnation, ministry, suffering and death of your true Son, our Saviour Jesus Christ. In his name we pray. Amen.

Retraining for the Middle-aged

God-Friend, today at the beginning of this retraining program
I pray for a double measure of your grace.

Once I used to look forward to such challenges, enthusiastic
about self-discovery, skill enhancement and new techniques.
But it is no longer that way. Now, in the middle years, I groan
at the imposition of yet another retraining, and I resent the
keen-eyed young gurus who will lead it.

Come to my aid, friend of those 'who labour and are over-
burdened'.

Marshal my inner resources, so that I will do much more than
merely endure these coming days. Awaken in me a youthful
spirit of adventure, and let it be tempered (not sat upon!) by
the wisdom of my middle years. Show me not only how to
better please my employers but also how to enhance my
performance as a servant of Christ both inside and outside the
place where I work.

God-Friend, I dedicate this training course to you. Again I pray
for a double measure of your grace. Through Jesus Christ our
Saviour. Amen.

Initiator

I would not have known
my name,
if You had not asked
it of me.

I would not have believed
my worth,
if You had not worn
my shame.

I would not have begun
to see,
if You had not lived
on this earth.

I would not have learnt
to love,
if You had not first
loved me.

An Elastic Love

O Lord, as years pass away and the heart shuts up and all things are a burden, let me never lose this youthful, eager love of you. Make your grace supply the failure of my nature. Do the more for me the less I can do for myself. Amen.

J H Newman (1801–90)

At Home in All Places

Not in a house, city or town,
    not in family, community or nation,
    but in you, God, we are at home.
When we rest our restlessness in you,
    we are at home at all times
    and in all places and situations.
Beneath the fraudulent glamour
    that disguises a godless society
    we find you loyally waiting for us.
When a bewildering gaggle of questions
    demand difficult answers from us,
    you are our sure starting point.
From the hard demands of the workplace
    for retraining or relocation,
    you are our refuge and strength.
When we are bruised by many knock-backs,
    and opportunities seem closed to us,
    yours is the door that is always open.
You, God! You, God of steadfast love,
    you are our immovable home,
    the hub of love and lasting joy! Amen!

For Special Gifts

Grace-giver, holy Friend, give us the sense to want you, the eagerness to seek you, the patience to wait for you, the insight to recognise you, the passion to meditate on you, and a lifestyle that praises you. Through the strength of the Spirit of Jesus Christ, our Lord. Amen.

St Benedict of Nursia (AD 480–547)

On Track

Lord of pilgrims,
when the track that looked promising
peters out and my energy is gone,
when all I can do is take shelter
from the chill wind,
    then I find you waiting
    with bread and wine
    and a hand on my shoulder,
    which turns me
    in a new direction
    where I never expected
    to travel.

Then as I set out,
surprised at the renovation
within my being,
delighted with the eagerness
which now spurs
my mind and feet,
I discover fresh tracks,
    new vistas to inspire me,
    new valleys and streams,
    new melodies on my tongue
    and new hopes that pray
    themselves into action.

Thanks, Lord of pilgrims,
for your renewing Spirit.
Amen.

Software

God of all power and truth and grace,
program us with the words and ways
of Nazareth's most famous Son,

that we may be able to configure
all the changes and pressures of this new age
with a wisdom that far exceeds self-interest
and with a love that outleaps all knowledge.

Through Christ Jesus, our Saviour. Amen.

Knock-backs

Lord of my life,

how often have I
begged you
    for special mercies,
besieged you
    for clear guidance,
pleaded for gifts
    with which to serve you,
knocked on your door
    like the pestering widow.

But time after time
    you have met me
with the grace
    of firm rejections,
and through these
    very knock-backs
you have taken me
    on a steeper track
    to a better destination.

For such hard love
and undiluted wisdom
    I give you rueful thanks
    and joyful praise!

For the Lukewarm

We, O God, we are the second-rate Christians.

We admire Jesus and follow him from a safe distance. We
know we need him yet are afraid to live on the frontiers of this
century with him. Those other enthusiastic Christians, who
wear their heart on their sleeve, embarrass us. Those who
openly evangelise or get all excited about their church, or who
are social justice activists, make us nervous. And so we drag
along half-believing, half-loving, half-living.

God of generous patience, save us from our caution. Help us
to break out of our timidity and take a few risks. Stir up in us
both the desire and the will to dare a little more each day. Let
us begin to enjoy the liberation of being fools for Christ's sake.
To your glory. Amen.

A Lost Christmas?

God! They have taken away Christmas
and we do not know where they have laid it!

They have replaced the Gift with an orgy of getting,
displaced Advent expectation with a pantomime of parties,
captured carols by candlelight and fed it to trivial television,
and drowned the Wonder in a swamp of alcohol.
We arrive at Christ's birthday distracted, distended,
disinterested.

Lord, Emmanuel, please lead us again to the place where
Christ is born, that we may come and worship him with the
delight of primitive adoration. Let this be, dear Lord. Let this
be! Amen!

Overload

It is too much, God!
Our brains feel battered by the growing avalanche.

Too many innovations, figures, opinions, warnings,
    promises, deceits, theories, and technical details.
    Enough is enough!
Yet we know that a selfish retreat is not the answer
    for those who follow the Saviour, Christ Jesus,
    through the competing complexities of this century.
Make us stayers, faithful God.
    Give us the will to say no to vain novelties
    and the wit to laugh at our own complaints.
Make us pray-ers, loving God.
    Give us the wisdom to discern your Spirit at work
    and the wish to boldly live by grace and truth.
And when we are utterly weary,
    give us time out with friends who dearly love you,
    in fellowship with Christ who makes all things new.
For yours is the kingdom,
the grace-full power and the only glory,
forever and ever. Amen.

Our Answer

Source of being,
Saviour of sinners,
Soul of new life,
    be our Answer
    in the scrum of life.

Source of being,
creating and shaping,
sustaining and tending,
    be our Answer
    when hope loses heart.

Saviour of sinners,
seeking and finding,
healing and freeing,
    be our Answer
    when love runs dry.

Soul of new life,
rebirthing and bonding,
inflaming and enlightening,
    be our Answer
    when faith burns low.

Source of being,
Saviour of sinners,
Soul of new life,
    be our Answer
    in life and death.

Shaping

You, God,
    who are shaping a glorious future
    out of the hazards and the opportunities
    of escalating changes and age-old convictions,
please give us more of your Spirit, so that we may discern
    between the good and evil of this tumultuous century
    and make those choices which will keep us within
    the currents of your life and light and holy joy.
Through Jesus Christ our Lord. Amen.

Keeping It Simple

God our Creator, I do not strive to understand you or the world
you have made. I cannot know the reason for pain and
suffering. I just want to relieve the pain and suffering of others.
I pray that as I do it, I may understand more clearly your nature:
that you are the father of all people, and that the hairs of my
head are numbered. Amen.

St Francis of Assisi (AD 1181–1226)

God, Our God

God, our God,
Creator, Redeemer, Inspirer,
we trust your mystery.

You are the end
    before the beginning,
the flower
    preceding seed.
You are the fruit
    before the tree,
the necessity
    within our need.
You are the purpose
    preceding patterns,
the pure word
    before all speech.
You are the meaning
    between the lines,
the finding
    before our seeking.
You are the past
    we cannot leave,
the pre-life
    that dies to live.

God, our God,
Creator, Redeemer, Inspirer,
we adore your mystery!

Awaiting Execution

I do not know, O God, what may happen to me today. I only know that nothing will happen to me but what has been foreseen by you from all eternity, and that is sufficient. O my God, keep me in peace. I adore your eternal designs. Through Jesus Christ our Lord. Amen.

Elizabeth of France (1764–94)

Old Proverbs

God of endless hope and enterprise, save us from old proverbs, which at times may discourage and shackle us.

Save us, merciful friend,
from not daring to rush in where angels fear to tread and thereby missing the opportunity of being a fool for Christ's sake;
from attempting to do today those things that are better put off until tomorrow;
from being stones that gather moss instead of becoming shiny in the activities of love;
from looking so carefully before we leap that our faith remains stuck in a pre-Easter timidity;
from believing that we only reap what we sow and so depriving ourselves and others of the bonus of amazing grace.

Loving God, make us free as the Wind and as bold as Christ, that we may offer this new age not a repetition of the past but a taste of that glorious future which you have in store for those who love you. Through Jesus Christ our Lord. Amen.

It's Not All up to Us

O my Lord, what a great comfort it is that you did not entrust the fulfilment of your will to one so useless as I! I thank you forever! Let all things praise you! As things stand, Lord, though my will is not yet free from self-interest, I freely hand it over to you. Amen.

St Teresa of Avila (1515–82)

In the Fast Lane

Lord of life, as your people become swept up
by the many accelerating changes
and challenges of these days,
help us to keep our balance.
Do not tolerate in your church
the easy options of knee-jerk negativity
or a comfortable compliance with the world.

Saturate our true-being with the unique gospel
of Christ Jesus, that we may not judge
by what our busy eyes see
or by what our ears hear.
Assist us to discern each day
the spiritual dimension running free
through all things, and to make choices
that will elevate humanity and glorify our God.

We do not ask you to make things easy for us
but that you keep us alert, true, loving
and joyful through these days
of remarkable happenings.
For yours is the emerging kingdom,
the renewing power, and the loving glory,
yesterday, today, tomorrow and forever! Amen!

First Things

Loving God, induce us to put first things first. Help us to see
that building a colony on Mars or growing replacement parts
for the human body does not make us more like you. By love
alone you lead us to our true destiny. Fill us with the tough,
tenacious, tender love of Christ Jesus, so that on Earth or on
Mars, in the biology lab or in the shopping mall, we may be
like you and serve you gloriously. For your love's sake. Amen.

Keep Us True

*Grant, Lord, that we may hold to you without parting, worship
you without wearying, serve you without failing, faithfully seek
you, happily find you, and forever possess you, the only God,
blessed now and forever. Amen.*

St Anselm (1033–1109)

Each Common Day

How wonderful, loving God,
    are your common gifts
    of time and place!
We go to our beds
    enfolded within
    the restful night.
A few hours later
    we awake to light
    and find ourselves
    in a perfectly new day
    never before explored
    or sullied by human shame.

May we, full-filled by Jesus Christ,
    who have found in each
    brief ordinary day
    a fifth dimension,
    explore and celebrate
    this inexpressible mystery
    by freely loving as we are loved.

Recycling

Creating God, teach us to use carefully the good gifts of this planet, our first home. Make us mindful of the hundreds of generations that might yet come, so that we minimise waste and recycle all we can.

We also pray for a recycling in our personal lives. By the grace of your Christ and the rejuvenation of your Spirit, recycle in us those gifts and virtues that may have become ragged or been cast aside.

Recycle our faith, that we may run and not be weary, walk and not faint.
Recycle our hope, that we may rise up from pessimism like the flight of eagles.
Recycle our love, that justice may roll on like a flood and righteousness like an everflowing stream.

Loving God, let us model our approach to recycling on your grace, which regards no gift as trivial and no person as redundant. For Christ's sake. Amen.

Changing Moods

Some summer evenings,
    when my body is hot and weary,
    my soul is subdued and sluggish,
    and my mind outcries
    against the gross stupidity,
    greed and cruelty
    of insolent humanity.
To believe in a God
who is love and beauty
seems sadly absurd.

But on a fresh morning,
    when my body rises young,
    while my mind and soul
    are delighted by magpies,
    thoughts of simple saints
    and the courageous Christ's
    remarkable sanity,
not to believe in a God
of loving immediacy
seems madly absurd.

Lord of great patience,
    to rest my tiny faith,
    my perceptions,
    my commitments,
    and my creeds,
    worship and service
in anything less
than the incarnate Word
is badly absurd.

Living in the Spirit

LIVING IN
THE SPIRIT

Spirit of Love

Spirit of Christ Jesus,
Spirit of living truth,
Spirit of peace and joy,
   we adore you.

You inflame prophets
   to fight injustices.
You infill saints
   with a unique beauty.
You infuse physicians
   with your compassion.
You instruct preachers
   to practise their preaching.
You inspire scientists
   to untangle secrets.
You increase the brave,
   who walk by faith.
You include the weak,
   whom the world despises.
You infect the strong
   with your gentle mercy.
You indwell all
   who share your cup.
You inflow the dead,
   and they come to life.

Love, you always were,
Love, you are today,
Love, you will ever be;
   we adore you.

Dear Wind

Wind over the waters,
Wind over the sea,
Wind of creation,
    breathe life in me.

Wind on the mountain,
Wind tossing the tree,
Wind of the prophets,
    breathe life in me.

Wind on the Jordan,
Wind on Galilee,
Wind at Golgotha,
    breathe life in me.

Wind full of Easter,
Wind of the free,
Wind of the gifted,
    breathe life in me.

Brain Scan

Spirit of truth, you have searched me and known me. You understand those quirks which even my best friends find off-putting. You scan the intricate circuitry of my brain and trace the subtle chemistry that influences my feelings and attitudes. There is not a thought in my head but you know it altogether. The secrets of my motivation are open to you. You indwell my soul-temple, where the gift of faith resides, resplendent among my doubts.

Spirit of searching intimacy, in your knowledge of me I find
    peace.
Spirit of unswerving truth, I rejoice in your faithfulness.
Spirit of Christ Jesus, I glory in your redemptive love.
Amen!

For Every Step Forward

We thank you, untiring Spirit of Truth, for every genuine step
forward made by the human race.

We give thanks for
    the increasing use of solar power
    the latest wonders of microsurgery
    new social skills in conflict resolution
    improved treatments for mental illness
    safer methods of pest control in agriculture
    every elimination of injustice and poverty
    a better understanding of the brain's chemistry
    the release of labourers from machine-like tasks
    new patterns in our worship, fellowship and service
    more Christian humility when dealing with other beliefs.

We thank you, recreating Spirit, that the past need not fetter
the future. We praise you that what eye has not yet seen or ear
yet heard, you have in store for those who love you. Through
Jesus Christ our ground and our goal. Amen.

Corellas at Dawn

Like doves,
a white cloud of corellas
descend on a dead tree,
turning a grey, damp dawn
into a thing of beauty.

Come, Spirit of love,
baptise the barren limbs
of our discouragement
with a flock of new hopes
and clothe our drabness
with your pure loveliness.

In your tough mercy
dig us out of our hiding places.
Touch our eyes with healing,
that we may look without hurt or fear
on that holy Light
which makes all things new.

Taking the Wind out of Our Sails

Holy Friend, we are ready for the challenges of this new era because of those times of grace when you have seemed to leave us, when you have taken the wind out of our sails and forced us to work hard against the tide. We complained often and at times feared that we were being carried backwards. But you had faith in us; you knew what we were capable of and waited for us to discover and develop the hidden strength with which your creating love endows us. For this hard mercy, and for your presence, hovering like a dove even when we thought we were alone, we thank and praise you, Holy Friend. Amen.

Fruits of the Spirit

(Galatians 5:22,23)

Giver of good gifts, as we accumulate an increasing array of microchip possessions and entertainments, do not let us forget the far more precious fruits of the Spirit.

Help us to treasure *love* far above all goods and services, and to
    open our hearts to a *joy* exceeding an adrenalin rush
    accept a *peace* not dispensed by pharmacies
    temper our frenetic busyness with *patience*
    replace heartlessness with *kindness*
    seek *goodness* much more than praise
    stay *faithful* when others grow faith-weary
    be *gentle* as doves in the markets of ruthlessness
    and show *self-control* in a casino-culture of self-indulgence.

Assist us to live well and love well, as friends of the Spirit who adopts us into the family of God. Fill us with yourself until no pocket of resistance or apathy remains and we become mirrors of Christ's abundant truth and grace. Amen.

The Dew

Pour on us, O Lord, the Spirit of love and family-kindness, that, sprinkled by the dew of your benediction, we may be made glad by your glory and grace. Through Jesus Christ our Lord. Amen.

Bone Valley

(Inspired by Ezekiel 37)

Save us, Breath of God,
as we pass through this century,
from seeing only the facade
of human pretension.
Please open our eyes
that we may find ourselves
in Bone Valley.

There, in this valley of death,
give us the courage
to preach to these bones,
that they may live.
If we protest our incapacity,
asking, 'How can we preach?
What word have we to say?'

remind us to preach
the Man of Nazareth:
words which mirror actions,
actions that mirror words,
a seamless robe,
love incarnate,
a faith that works.

Though we are inept
in the ways of such love,
help us to get started.
Then, as we speak, we will hear
some rattling as a few bones
come to life and stand up,
renewed in Christ Jesus.

Surely the Lord is in this place
though we did not know it!
We thank you, Breath of Hope,
that Bone Valley is most surely
becoming Easter Avenue,
where the dead hear the voice
of the Son of Love and live!

How Strange!

Wonderful God, how strange it is
that we sometimes cannot seem
to find you!

For without you we could not breathe one breath
or even have the air to breathe,
   without you no life or love,
   without you no light or joy,
   without you no beginning or end.

You are in all things and all are in you.
Our being flows from your holy Breath,
and to you we must return.

How strange it is that we lose our bearings
in the midst of such a remarkable, complete
and intimate love!

Wonderful God, glorify your name
even in our spiritual insensitivity
and times of unbelief! Amen.

The Making of Us

Creator-Spirit, you are the power which pulses beneath each
moment of our lives. We pray that our lives may resonate with
your purposes throughout each day.

As we push our way among the technology designed by human
brains, do not permit us to lose touch with your reality. May
we delight in the miracle of the human mind without bowing
down to it. Rather, let us honour that lofty Mind which is in
the process of making us. Keep alive in us the capacity to
wonder and worship and the desire to be inflooded with your
insatiable love.

Creator-Friend, in this early phase of the human story, go on,
we pray, with the difficult task of creating humanity, until we
enter into the glorious inheritance of the children of God.

By Your Spirit

When I am plunged into new situations
and want to impress peers
with my capacity to cope,
remind me, loving Lord,
that not by pride or power
but by your Spirit
are we fulfilled.

When I become infected and driven
by this tragic world's lust
for status and possessions,
tell me, loving Lord,
that not by pride or power
but by your Spirit
are we of worth.

When I feel wounded and betrayed
and want to hit out at others
to ease my pain and grief,
teach me, loving Lord,
that not by pride or power
but by your Spirit
are we healed.

When I want to take hold of events
and try to forcibly bend them
to make a better world,
show me, loving Lord,
that not by pride or power
but by your Spirit
are we renewed.

For your love's sake. Amen.

The Choirmaster of Life

*Heavenly Friend, the Encourager, the Spirit of Truth, you are
present in all places, filling all things. You are the treasury of
goodness, the choirmaster of life. Come and make your home
within us, clean out all dirt and wash our souls. Amen.*

St John Chrysostom (AD 347–407)

Sister of Dawn and Dusk

Sister of dawn and dusk,
  you are with us today.
God of childhood and old age,
  you are with us today.
Friend of the heavy-laden,
  you are with us today.
Spirit of the poor and merciful,
  you are with us today.
Joy of loving minds and hearts,
  you are with us today.
Love that will not let us go,
  you are with us always!

In God's Deep Space

God, our Creator and Saviour, set us adrift from those
handmade space stations which tempt the star explorer to give
up the search. Cut us off from the temptations of an easy life
within safe, rigid limits.

Encourage us to take love-risks, to journey deep into Spirit-
space. Help us to discover those new worlds which long ago
you prepared for us, when 'the morning stars sang together
and all the children of God shouted for joy'.

Through the grace of Jesus Christ, who is with us to the end of
all things. Amen.

Spirit Internet

Most generous God, you have chosen to make the internet of
your Spirit open to all who crave grace and truth. Encourage
us to surf through your resources without inhibition, willing to
knock and enter, seek and find, ask and receive.

Loving Friend, we want to access and express that special
cross-love which to the self-righteous is a stumbling block and
to the sophisticated is foolishness.

Through Christ Jesus our Saviour. Amen.

Cascade through Us

You, Spirit-Friend, who are the light of the dreary and the life
of the weary, rise up within us this day!
Leap up like the sun over dark valleys and enlighten both our
path and our minds.
Surge up like the springtime sap in vines and enliven our hands
for fruiting and our spirits for loving.
You, Spirit-Friend, who are older than the beginning and
younger than the end, cascade through us with your light and
life until we spill over with wonder, love and praise. Through
Jesus Christ our Lord. Amen.

DOING THE RIGHT THING

DOING THE RIGHT THING

~

Decisions!

Decisions, decisions, decisions! Creator God, help us! Spirit of truth, guide us! Jesus Christ, save us!

Although we find ourselves excited by the brilliant achievements of this new age, we become exhausted by its ethical challenges and confusions. There are moments, Lord, when we hanker for the simpler days of our great-grandparents, for whom the path of morality was simply defined by church authority. But now it seems as if our technological cleverness constantly outruns our ideas of goodness, and we cannot catch up.

Be with us, loving God, with all your compassion and wisdom. Be with us as we make decisions about genetic engineering and virtual reality, body transplants and performance-enhancing drugs, space exploration and the adventures of cyberspace, the artificial maintenance of life and euthanasia. Through all the changing scenes of life enable us to seek first your kingdom and its true-goodness.

Jesus Christ, make us as clever as serpents and as gentle as doves.
Spirit of Truth, keep us sharp-witted and love-directed.
Father of all mercies, help us to so trust you that all things may work together for good to those who love you.
For your love's sake. Amen.

Morality

Save us, compassionate God, from being sucked into the downward spiral of opinion-poll morality. Bear us upwards within the surging cycle of your grace, from the mediocre to the good, from the good to the better.

Put your divine discontent among our shabby thoughts and feelings, that we may hunger and thirst for that enlightened whole-iness which is your high calling through Christ Jesus our Lord. Amen.

For Some Help

Please give us, Father-God, a clean start for beginners, intelligence to the young, aid to those who are running hard, repentance to those who fall, a revived spirit to those who are lukewarm, and to those who have given their best a good ending. Amen.

St Irenaeus of Lyon (died AD 202)

To See Ourselves

Loving God, pity us when we imagine that our age is the most progressive and sophisticated that the world has known. We smirk at the half-truths and theories of superseded cultures, laugh at their fashions and fopperies, and are repelled by their wilful prejudice, which sustained grave injustices. In fact, we feel superior. We feel smug.

Have mercy on us, we pray. Give us the courage to assess ourselves as the future will assess us. Enable us to see through the deceits of our culture, to reject the myths that lead us astray, and to spurn the self-adulation which leaves no space for repentance and renewal.

Save us, redeeming Lord, from ourselves. Engulf us with your salvation. Nourish us with the Spirit and teaching of Christ Jesus. Let us live with his integrity and pass on to future generations some genuine fruits of your kingdom. To your glory and their enrichment. Amen.

Words

When it comes to words, we are a busy tribe, Lord. Every day we manufacture new words: new words to label our discoveries in biology and astronomy, new words for our latest medications and cosmetics, new words by the thousand to help us talk with computers, new words for this season's ice-cream and for flowers for our gardens—words, words, and yet more words!

Yet none of them bring us closer to you or to our neighbours. We are lost among our clever words.

Come to us and come into us with your one true Word! Come and make room for yourself among the clutter. Speak the Word that was with you from the beginning. Possess us and reshape us.

If we are too easily influenced, like clay in the hands of too many potters, take charge of us; by your word reshape us and fire us in the ovens of your mercy. If we have become like a road, hardened by the traffic of life, come with the jackhammer of your word to break us and remake us.

O Jesus Christ, incarnate Word, Friend and Saviour, enter us with the love that can redeem the lost and exceed our most daring expectations. To your glory and our profound happiness. Amen.

Who Are We?

Who are we, God? Pulled between the glittering allurements of this postmodern age and an ancient gospel of costly love, we try and serve two masters.

True God of True God, recall us to our first love and our primary commitment. Help us to define ourselves as children of light and joint-heirs with the one who loved us and gave himself for us. With our feet firmly on your ground, let us serve this postmodern world with compassion and courage.

Through Jesus Christ, the name above all others. Amen.

Genes and Choice

Lord of genes and chromosomes, how wonderfully you have made us! The more biologists decode the secrets that determine much of our physical and mental wellbeing the more cautious we become about praise and blame. We pray that we may be more humble about our own strengths and less judgmental about the failings of others.

Yet we give thanks for the critical component of liberty and responsibility which remains ours. We will choose this day whom we will serve. Let us use every opportunity to dignify life with those words and deeds which are grounded in love. Let us make each decision, from the smallest to the greatest, to praise and glorify your holy name. Through Jesus Christ our Lord. Amen.

Cloning?

We are uneasy, Lord of life. Although we share some of the excitement that follows the successful cloning of an animal, we have misgivings about what some person may attempt with human tissue. The possibility of megalomaniacs cloning themselves disgusts us as a new and terrible form of idolatry. To bow down and worship oneself seems to be the ultimate blasphemy. Deliver us, we pray, from the evil which insinuates itself into all human advancements. More than ever we need a Saviour who has overcome the 'world, the flesh and the devil'. Amen.

To Receive New Thoughts with Grace

Grant, O Lord God, that we may wait for the least hint of your will; that we may welcome all truth, under whatever outward forms it may be uttered; that we may have the grace to receive new thoughts with grace, recognising that your ways are not as our ways nor your thoughts as our thoughts; that we may bless every good deed, by whomsoever it may be done; that we may rise above all party strife and cries to the contemplation of the eternal Truth and Goodness, O God Almighty who never changes. Through Jesus Christ our Lord. Amen.

Charles Kingsley (1819–75)

The Ten Commandments

Save your people, God of truth and mercy,
from the chaos of divided loyalties
and the worship of many gods.
   Save us, God of truth and mercy.

From making God in our own likeness,
and from the slavery of self-centredness,
   save us, God of truth and mercy.

From using God's name trivially
and claiming him for our prejudices,
   save us, God of truth and mercy.

From neglecting sabbatical quiet times
and being obsessed with busyness,
   save us, God of truth and mercy.

From ignoring or despising the elderly
and overindulging the new generation,
   save us, God of truth and mercy.

From glorifying armaments and war
and wishing our enemies dead,
   save us, God of truth and mercy.

From watering down love and marriage,
and from the exploitation of sex,
   save us, God of truth and mercy.

From the legal robberies of the stock exchange
and the cunning thefts of tax evasion,
   save us, God of truth and mercy.

From TV programs that twist the facts,
and from cruel gossip in supermarkets,
   save us, God of truth and mercy.

From those who preach greed as a virtue,
and from possession-lust which is never satisfied,
   save us, God of truth and mercy.

O Jesus Christ, Saviour of all who lose their way,
O Healing Spirit, Power who renews the world,
   we need you, God of truth and mercy. Amen.

Wide-angle Lens

Loving God, assist us to work our way through complicated
issues. Fit our discernment with a wide-angle lens, that we may
see not only the immediate consequences for ourselves but also
the results of our actions at large. For your love's sake. Amen.

Voices

Great God of single-minded love, save us from the multiplicity
of faces and voices that crowd our senses and distract our
spirits.

From television sales-smiles and telephone patter which urge us
to store up treasure on earth,
   please deliver us, saving Friend.
From the latest well-marketed guru, recycling old delusions
and ancient heresies,
   please deliver us, saving Friend.
From arrogant scientists who pontificate on some new theory
as if it were eternal law,
   please deliver us, saving Friend.
From addiction to virtual reality and the bottomless pit of
internet pornography,
   please deliver us, saving Friend.
From electronic preachers who have so adapted Christianity to
serve the modern media that it has become mere consumer
goods,
   please deliver us, saving Friend.
From the much-publicised deeds of amoral superstars who
worship nothing but their own image,
   please deliver us, saving Friend.
From those politicians who are advertised as wise, caring
shepherds but are in fact egocentric wolves,
   please deliver us, saving Friend.
From an era that is obsessed with information and answers but
has forgotten the basic questions,
   please deliver us, saving Friend.

Blurred Edges

Lord of clarity,
here in this confusing century I find
the edges between faith and unbelief
are fudged and blurred.
This is your world;
I do not accept the easy doctrine
that it is all perverse and corrupt,
devoid of your works.

But where are you?

Where are the boundaries between
darkness and light, lie and gospel,
unfaith and bold faith?

God, my Saviour,
allow me neither to spurn your world
nor to be seduced by its tempting deceits
dressed up as truth.
Save me and guide me,
that it may not be said of my life,
Surely the Lord was in this place,
but you didn't know it.

Doubts

You who are the giver of faith
and understand the complexities
of the doubting mind,
come to us in the grace
of our risen Lord Jesus.
With his help
enable us to doubt
all our own doubts
with the same stringency
that we bring
to the blind credulity
and superstition
of others. Amen.

Among the Stars

Blessed are you, Joy of the universe!

Loving God, in this age of primitive space exploration we are beginning to realise that the future of humanity may fit somewhere among the stars. But morally and spiritually we are not ready for the mission.

We confess that evil is too much with us and of us. The thought of exporting our greed and aggression to other worlds sickens us. We confess that in spite of our science and technology we have not yet disciplined ourselves to cherish this earth and its vulnerable creatures. Although we can transplant hearts and manipulate genes, we are reluctant to act justly, love mercy and walk humbly with our God.

Please, God, do not let us loose on other worlds until we have learnt to care for this one. Help us to absorb quickly and thoroughly the ways of your True-Child, Christ Jesus. We long for more of his sanity in our politics, agriculture, commerce, education, recreation and scientific research.

Lord of the stars, not by our cleverness or our proud strength but by your Spirit shall we inherit that future which you have in store for those who love you.

Blessed are you, Joy of the universe! Amen and Amen!

ENJOYING RECREATION

ENJOYING RECREATION

Seamless Robe

God of an all-inclusive love,
help us to see the seamless robe
in which we live and move.

The cattle on a thousand hills
   the lilies of the field
a mother suckling her first-born
   the farmer tilling soil
sunshine breaking through nimbus clouds
   and rainstorms in the night
an athlete training in the dusk
   an old man tending vines
the desert carpeted with flowers
   an eagle on the wing
a pastor standing by a grave
   a nurse's skilful hands
the fish around a coral reef
   wagtails in wattle trees
anger against injustices
   repentance on its knees
a bridge that ends isolation
   a dam that conquers drought
children playing in autumn leaves
   a church singing with joy
the broken bread that nourishes
   the chalice that renews.

Creating and redeeming Love,
we reach out to your seamless robe
that we may touch and live. Amen.

Like a Video Game?

Lord of quietness, when we live frenetically, like figures on a video game, prompt us to make space for you. Let us long for a little peace, hunger for Christ's words, thirst for times of prayer and meditation.

Then, when all else rushes and glitters and babbles around us, let the overflow of your loveliness maintain a still centre in our being. From that quiet place, enlighten our decisions, direct our energies, and cool our overheated anxieties.

Hallow all our moments with a recognition of your perpetual presence and patience, to your praise and glory. Through Jesus Christ our Lord. Amen.

Time Out

Most loving God, we thank you that we can take time out from our busy existence to share those common experiences which have touched the tribes of this continent for thousands of years:

> time to walk in a forest among noble trees that soar towards the sunlight
> time to sit by a river at dusk and hear the anthems of kookaburras
> time to explore gravelly bushland and kneel to admire small ground orchids
> time to stand on a rocky headland and watch huge seas flinging high their white spumes
> time to witness the powerful grace of a red kangaroo leaping across a plain
> time to eat lunch under a rivergum and listen to the music of a stream
> time to stand waist-deep among wild boronia and inhale its fragrance
> time to venture at night under inland skies and marvel at the multitude of the stars.

Loving God, we thank you for these profound simplicities by which our anxieties are quietened, our wonder reawakened, and our spirits are renewed. We celebrate the Providence which has placed us in this ancient land. Wonderful is your name forever and ever! Amen.

City Life

Here in this city, God, where we are buffeted by noise and dependent on technology, it is difficult to have a sense of your presence. It is as if you don't exist.

Caught in our hectic schedules, we become agitated by the late arrival of a train, irritable with the slowness of an escalator, impatient with the measured responses of a computer.

We have lost the art of knowing you as Emmanuel, God-with-us always. So we rush on, blind to moments of beauty, insensitive to others, forgetting how to laugh, too busy for prayer, neglecting the grace of gratitude. God of Christ Jesus, open our eyes to see you and our hearts to love and worship you. Amen.

New-age Farmer

O new-age Farmer
   of persistent grace,
plough and harrow
   the barren fallows
of our discontent
   and faithlessness.

Come by day or night
   and sow our paddocks
with the mustard seeds
   of your own faith.
Send on these lands
   the sun and rain
that falls unstinted
   on good and bad alike,
until the germination
   erupts within us
and the wonder of greening
   transforms us all.

You, new-age Farmer,
   you alone we worship,
you who do not need us
   yet who take delight
in the clumsy praises
   of child, sinner and saint.
Hallelujah!

Come unto Me

(Matthew 11:28)

Jesus, our Messiah, we come to your divinity, which lies deeper than the beginning of the universe. We are drawn to you from the giddying activity of this microchip society, seeking your promised rest for tired and tattered human souls, and needing the recuperation offered by your Spirit.

O Child of humanity, O Child of God, in you we find a yoke that liberates and a burden that is light. You are life, love, joy and peace. You are beauty, strength and generous grace. You are the song that is new every morning, the melody that follows us to the long day's end.

Wonderful, wonderful, wonderful are you, sharer of burdens and wearer of human wounds! Glorious is your name forever and ever! Amen.

Things That Endure

Loving God, we who spend our years among innovations and revolutions give thanks for the humble things of this continent which preceded our birth and will long outstay us:

> the great rock of Uluru, rainforests of the Franklin;
> moonlight on Gippsland Lakes, tides washing Sydney harbour;
> wildflowers of the West, snowfields of the South-East;
> eagles over Wilpena Pound, wombats on the Nullarbor plain;
> coral gardens of the Barrier Reef, waterlilies of Kakadu lagoons;
> the sunrise of each morning, the Cross among the evening stars.

For these long-lasting reminders of a Creator's providence and, best of all, for the Spirit of Christ whose love is more permanent than creation, we, the temporary inhabitants of this land, give you our gratitude and praise. Amen.

Don't Worry

Loving God, rescue us from the acidic worries which eat away the serenity of those who have divided aims. Save us from being bullied or manipulated by the latest fashions in clothing or computers, food or motor cars, entertainment, housing or religion.

Return us to the sanity of trusting you unconditionally. Open our eyes to the beauty of wildflowers and the freedom of bush ravens, who can do nothing but rely on providence. Help us to glory in your providential grace and relax our frayed lives into your immense salvation.

God of Christ Jesus and our God, garrison our souls with the peace which passes all understanding. For your love's sake. Amen.

For Travellers

Pilgrim God,
    on those inland journeys
when our faith
    seems a dry saltpan
and our prayers
    a cloud of bulldust,
open within us
    the gift of remembrance.

Stir our minds
    to remember your visitations:
fresh springs
    we found in barren places;
wild peaches
    we enjoyed in a rocky gorge;
the shade
    we sought beside a rock;
a honeyed tree
    growing in desert sands;
the stranger
    who joined us on the road;
and the joy that came
    from a damper shared
    and a cup passed around.

Teach Us

*Lord, teach us to seek you, for we cannot seek you unless
you teach us or find you unless you show yourself to us.
Let us seek you in our desiring and desire you in our seeking.
Let us find you by loving you and love you when we find you.
Through Jesus Christ our Lord. Amen.*

St Anselm (1033–1109)

Simple Things

Keep us in touch, good Lord, with the enduring, simple
pleasures of life. Though we are cluttered around with plastic
surfaces and microchip wizardry, give us an awareness of the
glory to be found in common things:

> the smell of the bush after summer rain
>> a chuckle from an infant playing on the floor
> a well-earned rest under a shady tree
>> the wisdom of the aged, offered with a smile
> the sound of the surf rolling on sandy shores
>> the aroma of scones, newly baked
> a welcome swallow nesting under the eaves
>> the feel of warm soil as we plant seedlings
> a word of encouragement from a stranger
>> the embrace of a friend in the hour of sorrow
> a platypus busy in a clear stream
>> an evening breeze at the end of a hot day
> the juiciness of fruit freshly picked
>> the scent of rain after a drought
> a phrase from Jesus in a moment of doubt
>> the sight of a table, spread for us
> the fragrance of wine, poured out for us.

Keep us in touch, good Lord, with your gifts that are as old as
faith yet new every morning. Through Jesus Christ our Lord.
Amen.

Love That Surfs

Love,
that surfs the internet
of turbulent time
and says,
You are saved;
become what you are.

Love,
the first of all loves
and the final love,
wider than time,
that says,
You are mine;
I have called you by name.

Love,
the undiluted joy
at the nucleus
of each moment,
saying,
Come unto me;
I will give you rest.

Love,
the best wedding wine
kept until the last
sparkling hour,
saying,
My cup runs over;
drink, all of you.

Love,
the costly love
exceeding price
yet shared by beggars,
that says,
I am with you always,
to the end of the world.

Friend of Boat People

Friend of boat people, come looking for us in harbours where we hesitate in timidity and anxiety. Pilot us through the shallows and miseries of indecision to the deep ocean of faith.

Give us the wisdom to set our course by the star of Bethlehem and keep our tiller true. Whether we are running with the wind or beating into it, give us the courage of our convictions. On dark nights when the storm roars, let us hear your voice saying, 'Fear not. It is I.'

Bring us to that future which is far less than our avaricious wants and infinitely more than our holiest expectations.

To your eternal praise and glory. Amen.

Living Longer?

I have come that you may have life, and have more of it.

Father of the Christ who went where none had dared go before, guide us towards the fullness of life.

When the scientific prophets tell us that in this brave century people will be enabled live much longer, maybe to the age of a hundred and fifty years, we are uneasy. Is that what you, God, most want for us? For that matter, is that what we want for ourselves?

Merely continuing on here, seeing the world repeat its old sins, gives us scant enthusiasm. Some of us, loving God, are weary of recycling our past mistakes. We look for a greater redemption than a delaying of our ageing. We want to treasure that gift of quality-life which Jesus showed in his ministry and sealed through his death and resurrection.

Merciful Friend, let us live long or die tomorrow, but please keep us in the upsurge of the eternal life which has broken into time and embraces us today. This is life—the real thing! It is joy, peace, abundance. It is immortality. Praised be your name forever! Amen.

The Old That Is New

We are grateful, eternal God, for those old Bible words and images which still speak to us of your bonus-goodness, which is always one step ahead of us:

for the wind, blowing when and where it will, which rustles our curtains at evening;
for the impudence of that peculiar faith which asks us to plant a tree in the midst of the sea;
for the deep-rooted true vine, heavily pruned so that it may bear much more fruit;
for special moments when tongues of fire leap in this world's shame and gloom;
for the ravens and currawongs, who neither sow nor reap yet manage to be well fed;
for the spring of living water, which washes much deeper than the flow from our taps;
for the hand holding the lamp which goes searching in the darkness for one lost coin;
for the cup, full and running over, which is prepared for the least, the last and the lost.

Eternal God, intimate Friend, we rejoice in the unexpected, undeserved, unconditional love which has nurtured generations before us and will be faithful to all the generations that are to come. Through Christ Jesus our brother and teacher. Amen.

Not Far to Go

It is not far to go
    for you are near.
It is not far to go
    for you are here.
And not by travelling, Lord,
    we come to you,
but by the way of love,
    and we love you.

Amy Carmichael (1868–1951)

The New Science

We give thanks, ever-creative Spirit, for the new wave of
philosopher-scientists who challenge old secular orthodoxy.
We give thanks for the movement away from the scientific
dogmatism of the modern era towards a greater openness and
humility.

We give thanks for those
who demonstrate that in this universe all things are
interrelated and that nothing is insignificant;
who observe an 'uncertainty principal' applying everywhere,
with nothing fixed and final in creation itself;
who tell us that all our boasted 'objective' experiments are
influenced by our subjective human minds and
interventions;
who claim that because of an element of surprise, what we
do today does not exclusively determine tomorrow;
who assert that neither our minds nor our instruments can
ever predict the shape of the future;
who believe that the basic nature of all things is more like
relationship than mechanics;
who warn that we cannot be objective or sit on the fence,
for we are inextricably a part of all that is coming to be;
who suggest that awe and wonder are more appropriate
responses to this universe than pompous pronouncements;
who live their days aware of an elemental mystery at the
heart of all things.

We thank you, Spirit of Truth, for this new intellectual
modesty. We pray that as Christians we may play our part in
this emerging scene by listening, questioning, witnessing,
praying, knowing the Scriptures, worshipping, and humbly
serving our neighbours with a humility like that of the Son of
God. In whose name we pray. Amen.

The Best Gift of All

(Based on 1 Corinthians 13)

Even though we can listen to music as it is being played in Vienna, London or Tokyo, although we can hold conversations with astronauts in space, if these achievements are without God-love, they remain mere noise. Even though we should predict the birth of stars, unravel the mystery of antimatter, understand every gene, and have a faith that shifts mountains on Mars, yet if we are without God-love, we are worth nothing.

God our Creator and Saviour, give us your unique love, that we may be patient and kind, without jealousy or boastfulness. Replace our selfishness with your love, until our irritability, resentment and gloating give way to celebrating the saving truth. Fill us with your love that we may bear all things, believe all things, hope all things and outlive all things.

God, we fall far short of our destiny. Our knowledge is flawed, our prophetic insight is blurred. We are but children looking into a dirty mirror.

Help us, God, to begin to understand you in the same way as you understand us. Let us really believe (and trust our all to this creed) that faith, hope and love are eternal, with God-love the best of all. Through Jesus Christ our Lord. Amen.

www.ingramcontent.com/pod-product-compliance
Lightning Source LLC
Chambersburg PA
CBHW032037040426

42449CB00007B/927